SOUTH CAROLINA'S
Revolutionary War Battlefields

SOUTH CAROLINA'S

Revolutionary War Battlefields

A TOUR GUIDE

R. L. Barbour

PELICAN PUBLISHING COMPANY

Gretna 2002

*This guide is in memory of and
dedicated to Arnold G. Stewart*

*The word "Pelican" and the depiction of a pelican are trademarks
of Pelican Publishing Company, Inc., and are registered
in the U.S. Patent and Trademark Office.*

Library of Congress Cataloging-in-Publication Data

Barbour, R. L.
   South Carolina's revolutionary war battlefields : a tour
guide / R.L. Barbour.
       p. cm.
   Includes bibliographical references and index.
   ISBN 1-58980-008-7 (pbk.)
       1. South Carolina—History—Revolution, 1775-
   1783—Battlefields—Guidebooks. 2. Historic sites—
   South Carolina—Guidebooks. 3. South Carolina—Tours.
   4. United States—History—Revolution, 1775-1783—
   Battlefields—Guidebooks. I. Title.

E263.S7 B36 2002
973.3'09757—dc21

                                                    2001059823

*Photographs by author
Maps by Tim Belshaw*

Printed in the United States of America
Published by Pelican Publishing Company, Inc.
1000 Burmaster Street, Gretna, Louisiana 70053

Contents

Preface and Acknowledgments

When Americans think about the Revolutionary War, minutemen and Massachusetts automatically come to mind. In fact, more Revolutionary War battles took place in South Carolina than in any other state. Approximately 250 battles and engagements can be documented, although some historians estimate the figure to be closer to 300. And this is just armed conflicts. The number of American Revolutionary War-related sites is much higher. Put simply, South Carolina is to the Revolution what Virginia is to the War for Southern Independence.[1]

Of the 250 battle sites in South Carolina, about 100 are documented well enough to be locatable today. As you might guess, many sites have been lost to urbanization and development. Others are deep in a woods or out in a cotton field; a few are under the waters of one of the state's manmade lakes; many are on private property. The sites included in this guide were chosen based on three criteria: they are associated with a good battle story, they are accessible by car or on foot, and there is something to see when you get there. In one case, no battle took place at the site—Francis Marion's grave. As you visit battle sites, you will become familiar with General Marion and his exploits. He is such an important figure in South Carolina's history that his final resting place could not be overlooked, and the exception seemed justified.

Serious students can appreciate the past simply through the written word. For most people, however, history truly comes alive when one can be physically present at the location where an event took place. This guide is for serious students, casual sightseers, and everyone in between.

In the process of conducting research for this book, I drew upon the resources of a valuable yet largely untouched source—county historical societies and the local historians associated with them. I owe a debt of gratitude to all those who assisted me in locating battle sites and who opened their counties' collections to me. I would especially like to thank Rick Hatcher, chief historian, Fort Moultrie/Fort Sumter National Monument; Dr. Stephen R. Wise, curator of the museum at the United States Marine Corps Recruit Depot, Parris Island, South Carolina; Wofford E. Malphrus and Curtis Smart, Jasper County Historical Society; Horace Rudisill, Darlington County; Tommy Lett, curator, Marion County Museum; Susan Starnes, South Carolina Cotton Museum, Bishopville; Agnes Corbett, Camden Archives & Museum; Laurie Robinson, director, Old Edgefield District Archives; Jackie Bartley, Aiken County Historical Museum; Ellen Jenkins, Barnwell County Public Library; Bob Edmunds, McCormick County; Eric K. Williams, chief park ranger, Ninety Six National Historic Site; Arnold Stone, Newberry County; David George, Laurens County; Chris Revels, chief park ranger, Kings Mountain National Military Park; Wade B. Fairey, executive director, Historic Brattonsville; Hurley Badders, Pendleton District Historical and Recreation Commission; Mike Foley, South Carolina Department of Parks, Recreation & Tourism; and Ty Houck, park superintendent, Old Dorchester State Park.

How to Use This Guide

This guide will lead you to South Carolina's Revolutionary War battlefields. It is neither a comprehensive history of that war nor of any of the battles included herein. To further your knowledge of the subject, refer to the bibliography at the end of this guide for more reading material.

These battle synopses are meant to be read on site, although the five National Park Service sites all have visitor centers with orientation films, exhibits, maps, and ranger programs that will be integral to your visit.

Although the war spanned nearly seven years, most of the battles in South Carolina took place in 1780 and 1781. However, the terminology, rather than the dates, seems to cause the most difficulty for students of the war. Troops were known by their military, political, national, and colloquial nomenclature. Here, then, is a simple chart to help keep them straight:

American	*British*
Patriots	Loyalists
Whigs	Tories
Militia and Continentals	Redcoats

Bear in mind that the Loyalists were Americans fighting for the British, whereas the Patriots were fighting for independence *from* the British.

You will be visiting four types of sites: 1) National Park Service sites at major battlefields, 2) historic towns and villages, primarily Brattonsville and Camden (an NPS affiliate), 3) state parks/sites such as Eutaw Springs, Fort Dorchester, and Francis Marion's grave, and 4) bridges and ferries, where many encounters took place due to the fact that troops became bottlenecked at river crossings, making them easy targets for the enemy.

The sites in this book are arranged chronologically by the date of the engagement. The dates of some battles are uncertain. The date found in the majority of sources is listed in this guide for each site. American commanders are listed first; British commanders are listed after the semicolon. Abbreviations for casualties are as follows: k—killed, w—wounded, c—captured, m—missing. Directions to each site begin with a city or town that can be found on the state highway map distributed free of charge at South Carolina Welcome Centers and published by the Department of Transportation. The abbreviation "SR" in the directions indicates a state road.

State highway markers are found at or near many sites. A guide to those markers is available from the South Carolina Department of Archives and History. Some of these markers have been knocked down or are missing. Therefore, the granite markers placed by the Daughters of the American Revolution are more reliable. These markers are the focal point of many of the battle sites you will visit on your journey throughout the beautiful and historic state of South Carolina.

A word of warning is in order to all who visit these sites. Your journey will take you through woods, fields, swamps, creeks, lakes, and rivers. While you admire the beauty, always be mindful of where you are walking. South Carolina is home to many varieties of snakes, some of them poisonous. Although snake bites are rare, look before you step. Also, alligators abound in the lowcountry—the area from the coast up to Lake Marion. As wild animals, they generally keep their distance from people. However, *do not*, under any circumstances, feed an alligator. This may provoke an attack not only from that particular alligator but from its future progeny as well, as over time these animals will associate people with food. And finally, you will be traveling along many dirt roads of varying condition. If you are driving a vehicle with low clearance, be careful where you drive, stop, and park. Assistance may not be readily or easily available if you are far off the beaten track. Common-sense precautions will help you enjoy your Revolutionary adventure!

SOUTH CAROLINA'S
Revolutionary War Battlefields

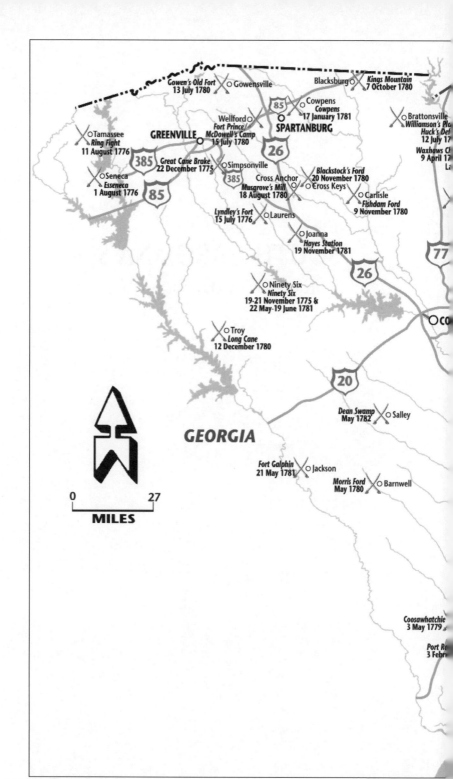

Gowen's Old Fort
13 July 1780 O Gowensville
Blacksburg O Kings Mountain
7 October 1780

Wellford O Cowpens
Fort Prince/ Cowpens
McDowell's Camp 17 January 1781
15 July 1780 SPARTANBURG

O Tamassee Brattonsville
Ring Fight Williamson's Pla
11 August 1776 Huck's Def
12 July 17

GREENVILLE Waxhaws CI
9 April 17
La

385 Great Cane Brake O Simpsonville
22 December 1775

O Seneca Blackstock's Ford
Esseneca Cross Anchor 20 November 1780
1 August 1776 Musgrove's Mill O Cross Keys
85 385 18 August 1780 O Carlisle
Fishdam Ford
9 November 1780

Lyndley's Fort O Laurens
15 July 1776

O Joanna 77
Hayes Station
19 November 1781

O Ninety Six 26
Ninety Six
19-21 November 1775 &
22 May-19 June 1781 O CO

O Troy
Long Cane
12 December 1780

20

Dean Swamp O Salley
May 1782

GEORGIA

Fort Galphin O Jackson
21 May 1781

Morris Ford O Barnwell
May 1780

Coosawhatchie
3 May 1779

Port Re
3 Febr

0 ———— 27
MILES

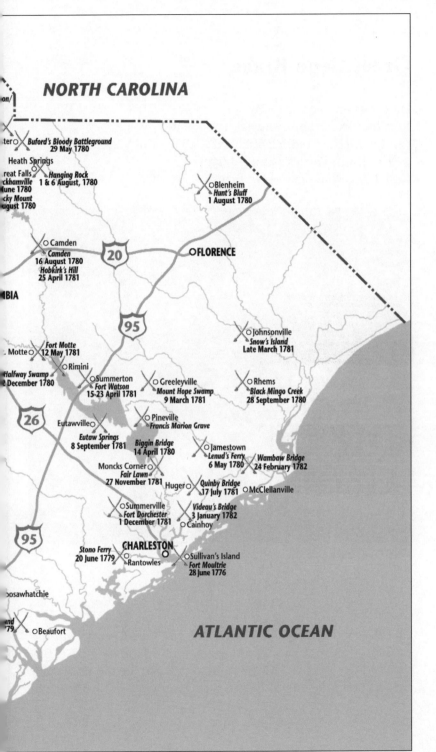

NORTH CAROLINA

ter○ Buford's Bloody Battleground
29 May 1780

Heath Springs

reat Falls
ckhamville ×Hanging Rock
une 1780 1 & 6 August, 1780

cky Mount
ugust 1780

×Blenheim
Hunt's Bluff
1 August 1780

○ Camden
Camden
16 August 1780
Hobkirk's Hill
25 April 1781

○FLORENCE

BIA

Fort Motte
. Motte○ ×12 May 1781
○Rimini

×Johnsonville
Snow's Island
Late March 1781

Halfway Swamp
2 December 1780
○Summerton ×Greeleyville
Fort Watson Mount Hope Swamp
15-23 April 1781 9 March 1781

○Rhems
Black Mingo Creek
28 September 1780

Eutawville× ×○Pineville
Eutaw Springs Francis Marion Grave
8 September 1781 Biggin Bridge
14 April 1780
○Jamestown
Lenud's Ferry
6 May 1780 Wambaw Bridge
×24 February 1782

Moncks Corner○
Fair Lawn
27 November 1781 Huger○ ○Quinby Bridge
17 July 1781 ○McClellanville

○Summerville
Fort Dorchester
1 December 1781 Videau's Bridge
3 January 1782
○Cainhoy

Stono Ferry **CHARLESTON**
20 June 1779 × ○
×Rantowles ○Sullivan's Island
Fort Moultrie
28 June 1776

osawhatchie

nd
79 × ○Beaufort

ATLANTIC OCEAN

Great Cane Brake

Date: December 22, 1775
Location: Near Simpsonville, Greenville County
Commanders: Colonels Richard Richardson, William
   Thomson; Patrick Cunningham
Casualties: American—1w; British—5k, 130c

Great Cane Brake.

Years before any significant penetration of British Redcoats into the upcountry, acute factionalism spurred conflict here. The Provincial Congress, whose delegates were leaders in the cause for liberty, first met in Charleston in January 1775. They ordered Col. Richard Richardson to "silence the discontents of the backcountry" and "deliver up the bodies of all principal offenders"—those still loyal to the British government. By mid-December he had gathered a formidable force of over 4,000 and they were hot on the heels of the elusive Tory leader, Patrick Cunningham. Richardson learned he was camped near the Cherokee lands on the Reedy River and sent a detachment of 1,300 men under Col. William Thomson on an all-night, 25-mile march in pursuit. The Patriots attacked the sleeping Loyalists at the break of dawn. Cunningham jumped out of bed, mounted his horse bareback, and shouted to his men to "shift" for themselves as he narrowly escaped to the Indian lands. Due to the cool-headedness and restraint of Colonel Richardson, few Loyalists were killed, but the Patriot victory netted 130 prisoners as well as much-needed supplies, arms, and ammunition.

Directions: From Fountain Inn (or I-385), take Hwy. 418; 1.6 miles past the intersection with SR 55 (Fairview Rd.), turn right onto South Harrison Bridge Rd. The highway marker is 0.7 mile on the left. From Greenville, take Exit 26 off I-385 (Harrison Bridge Rd., SR 453), turn right at the end of the ramp, proceed 2.6 miles, bear left onto North Harrison Bridge Rd., cross over New Harrison Bridge Rd. (SR 542), and proceed on South Harrison Bridge Rd. for just over 1 mile to highway marker on the right. The actual battle site is unknown, as it was a "running battle," but is close to the creek and now on private property.

Fort Moultrie

Date: June 28, 1776
Location: Sullivan's Island, Charleston County
Commanders: Col. William Moultrie; Sir Henry Clinton,
    Adm. Peter Parker
Casualties: American—10k, 22w; British—64k, 141w

Fort Moultrie. Palmetto trees, like those in the foreground, were used in the construction of the original fort.

Brought to a virtual standstill in the North by the brilliant generalship of George Washington, the British now turned their attention southward. Upon learning of a vulnerable, unfinished fort on Sullivan's Island at the entrance to Charleston harbor, Sir Henry Clinton ordered a two-pronged attack. He would land his forces on Long Island (northeast of Sullivan's, now Isle of

Palms), ford Breach Inlet, and attack the fort by land from the rear, while Adm. Peter Parker's fleet of nine warships bombarded the fort from the water. Although work on the fort had been proceeding furiously for months, only two walls and two bastions were complete; the two rear walls were only seven feet high. Inside were a little over 400 troops of the Second Regiment under the command of Col. William Moultrie. Even Moultrie admitted that if the British were able to sail past the fort and fire on the unprotected rear, all would be lost.

The first shots rang out around 10 a.m. Much to everyone's surprise, even well-placed British shells were largely ineffective due to the fort's unique construction. Building materials consisted of those materials readily available—sand, and logs hewn from the palmetto trees found in abundance on the island. The wood of these trees has the unusual characteristic of being soft and spongy, and when the cannonballs hit, the wood simply yielded, rather than splintering like hardwood and throwing dangerous projectiles into the defenders.[1] Shells landing in the sand were equally ineffective; most never even ignited. On the other hand, Moultrie was short of ammunition from the beginning, and although supplies were sent during the battle, he had enough to fire each gun only about once every 10 minutes. Each shot had to count. At one point Moultrie had to cease fire completely for nearly an hour. As the British warships continued the attack, the regimental flag, blue with a white crescent, was shot down and fell outside the walls of the fort. Ignoring the enfilading fire, Sgt. William Jasper retrieved the flag, affixed it to a sponge staff, and, mounting the parapet, shouted, "Don't let us fight without a flag."

Meanwhile, things were going poorly for Clinton on Long Island. He had been informed that the breach could easily be forded but, having failed to conduct his own reconnaissance, found the shallowest point to be seven feet deep and 75 yards across a swiftly moving current. He was eventually able to ferry some of his men across in several small boats, but the Third Regiment, under the command of Col. William Thomson, was ready and waiting for him. A company of South Carolina sharpshooters easily picked off the Redcoats as they tried to cross.

Exasperated at his lack of progress, Admiral Parker soon ordered three of his ships through the channel and past the fort. There they ran aground on a sandbar; two even collided with one another in an effort to free themselves.[2] And while Clinton was suffering from "unspeakable mortification" at his predicament, Parker was experiencing his own embarrassments. He was wounded by one of the well-placed shots from the fort and had the "hind part of his breeches shot away, which laid his posteriors bare."[3] The battle finally ended at dusk.

All told, the British lost 64 killed and 141 wounded, including South Carolina's royal governor, William Campbell, who would die of his wound two years later in England. Patriot casualties numbered 10 killed and 22 wounded. The British fleet withdrew in a crushing defeat. The situation would be dramatically different when they returned to Charleston a year later.

Directions: From Charleston, cross the Cooper River bridge on Hwy. 17 towards Mt. Pleasant. Take the Coleman Blvd. exit to Hwy. 703 onto Sullivan's Island, turn right, and proceed to the southern end of the island. The National Park Service entrance is on the right. After you visit the fort and Visitor's Center, turn left out of the parking lot and drive to the northern tip of the island. This bridge crosses Breach Inlet.

Lyndley's Fort

Date: July 15, 1776
Location: Near Laurens, Laurens County
Commanders: Majors Andrew Williamson, Jonathan Downs
Casualties: British—2k, 13c

While British strategy in the South Carolina upcountry depended largely on their ability to recruit Loyalist Americans, they wasted no time in allying Indians to the Crown. To counter this effort, a group of Patriots under the command of Maj. Andrew Williamson moved gradually throughout the backcountry, gathering various detachments as they went along. On the night of July 15, a party of 150 soldiers on their way to join Williamson stopped to fortify a small group of settlers who had taken refuge at Lyndley's Fort. The next morning, the fort was attacked by 88 Indians and 102 white Loyalists, some of whom were dressed and disguised as Indians and who were unaware of the soldiers within. Not only were the attackers repulsed, but the Patriots, led by Maj. Jonathan Downs, pursued and captured a number of them.

Directions: From Laurens, take Hwy. 252 west approximately 5 miles, turn left onto SR 398 (Ft. Lindley Rd.), and go 2 miles to the highway marker on the left. The battle site is on private property but can be seen from the road.

Esseneca

Date: August 1, 1776
Location: Seneca Old Town, Pickens County
Commanders: Maj. Andrew Williamson, Col. LeRoy
  Hammond; Alexander Cameron
Casualties: American—3k, 14w

Fort Rutledge. The stockade-shaped monument is located near the site of the battle at Esseneca.

In the early days of the war, the terms "Indian troubles" and "civil war" took on whole new meanings as Patriots and Loyalists each vied for the allegiance of the Cherokees. At Lyndley's Fort, white Loyalists, dressed and painted as Indians, fought alongside the Cherokees in an attack against Patriot soldiers and settlers. Maj. Andrew Williamson, who had been in

20

command of the Patriots at Ninety Six, planned an attack on Alexander Cameron, the British Indian agent who was camped on Onconore Creek, but the Indians were waiting for Williamson and his men as they crossed the Keowee River at Esseneca. Positioning his forces in houses and behind fences and trees, Cameron caught the Patriots by surprise and was easily able to rout them. Major Williamson's horse was shot out from under him, but the day was saved by Col. LeRoy Hammond, who rallied about 20 men and ordered them to charge the fence where the heaviest fire was coming from. The Indians were so startled by the sudden turn of events that they dropped their arms and fled into the woods. After the battle, numerous Indian towns on the frontier fell to the Patriot forces stationed at Fort Rutledge, which was built soon after this battle.

Directions: From Clemson take Hwy. 76 towards Anderson, and turn right onto Old Stone Church Rd. (look for signs to the SC Dept. of Natural Resources), which becomes Cherry Rd. Following the signs to the Madren Conference Center, turn left onto Old Stadium Rd. and left into the conference center and inn complex. Turn right onto the service access road that leads towards the pumping station. Cross over the dike and park just past the third building on the right (the one closest to the road). Walk straight ahead into the woods for approximately 50 yards to the Fort Rutledge Monument.

Ring Fight

Date: August 11, 1776
Location: Near Tamassee, Oconee County
Commanders: Col. Andrew Pickens; Cherokee Indians
Casualties: American—6k, 17w; Indians—16k

Ring Fight. Gen. Andrew Pickens built his home near the site of this battle.

With Indian uprisings on the frontier, Col. Andrew Pickens was sent with his militia troops to the upcountry. While Pickens was leading a party of 25 men through an old Indian field, they were attacked by 185 Cherokees, who surrounded the Patriots in a circular or ring formation, typical of their style of warfare. Swift and skillful marksmanship by the Patriots inflicted heavy casualties. But legend has it that a nearby canebrake was set afire, and as the moist reeds filled with steam and burst, they exploded with a loud popping noise that sounded like gunfire. The effect magnified the actual rifle fire and the Indians fled in confusion. Pickens' brother Joseph soon arrived with reinforcements, but the battle was already won. Andrew Pickens was so impressed by the beauty of the area that he later settled here.

Directions: From Tamassee, take SR 32 west to SR 172; turn right onto SR 375 and left onto SR 95. The monument to General Pickens' home where he died in 1817 is approximately 0.5 mile on the right, just past the intersection of Jumping Branch Rd. The exact location of the battle is unknown, but it took place close to this location.

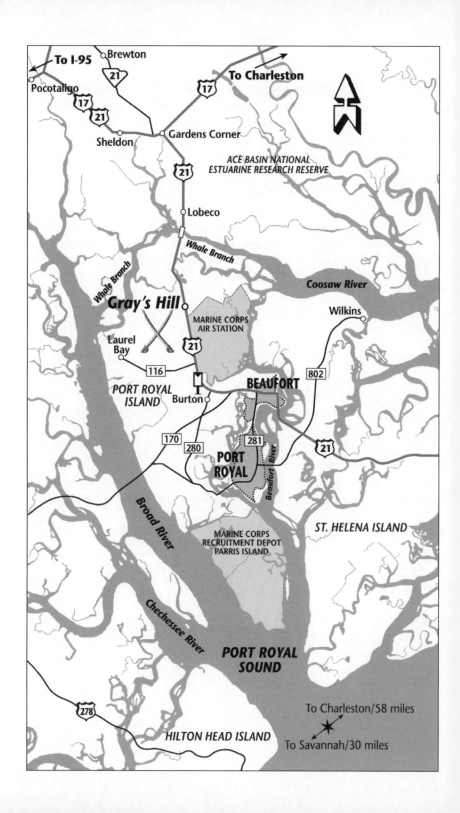

Port Royal Island

Date: February 3, 1779
Location: Near Beaufort, Beaufort County
Commanders: Col. William Moultrie; Maj. Gen. Augustine
  Prevost
Casualties: American—7k, 25w; British—75k & w

Having captured Savannah on December 29, 1778, Maj. Gen. Augustine Prevost now set his sights on Charleston. The British had failed to take the city in June 1776 at the Battle of Sullivan's Island (later called Fort Moultrie), and now the hero of that battle, Col. William Moultrie, was placed in command of the Beaufort militia and it was his task to stop the British advance. Prevost had sent a detachment of 150 troops under Major Gardner from Tybee Island, near Savannah, on four transport ships with two gunships escorting them.

The British infantry was landed on the northwestern tip of Port Royal Island and made contact with Moultrie's men about halfway between Port Royal Ferry and Beaufort. Moultrie had been looking to establish his line near the cover of the brush and the swamp but found the area already in possession of the British, a reverse of the usual situation. Major Gardner approached the Patriots, sword drawn, and demanded that Colonel Moultrie surrender his forces.

Refusing, Moultrie had his artillery open fire, and battle raged hot and heavy for approximately an hour.[1] With his supply of ammunition nearly exhausted, Moultrie ordered a withdrawal but, much to his surprise and delight, found the British already in retreat for the same reason. With little ammunition between them, both sides retreated. Moultrie led his forces to the American base at Purrysburgh, about 30 miles to the west on the Savannah River. Unable to capture Port Royal Island, the British plundered plantations along the Broad River on their retreat to Savannah.

Directions: Take Hwy. 17 south to Hwy. 21 east towards Beaufort. Cross the bridge at Whale Branch. The next light (at SR 71) is the crest of Gray's Hill, where the battle took place. The highway marker is several miles beyond this at a picnic site on the right, just in front of the water tower (1 mile north of the Marine Corps Air Station entrance).

Coosawhatchie

Date: May 3, 1779
Location: Coosawhatchie, Jasper County
Commanders: Colonels William Moultrie, John Laurens; Gen.
  Augustine Prevost
Casualties: American—3k, 8w

Despite the defeat at Port Royal Island, General Prevost was determined to make a second attempt to capture Charleston. Instead of a small detachment of 150 men, this time he crossed the Savannah River with 2,400 British regulars, and once again, William Moultrie stood in his way. This time, however, Moultrie was outnumbered two to one. He determined to make a stand on a slight ridge at the Tullifinny River, about 2 miles east of the Coosawhatchie River, where he left about 100 men to guard the crossing and warn him of the Redcoats' arrival. As the enemy drew near, Moultrie was about to send an aide to pull these troops back to the main force when Col. John Laurens offered to lead them back. Moultrie had so much confidence in the officer that he sent along 250 men to help cover the flanks. In direct disobedience of orders, Laurens crossed the river and formed the men in line for battle. He failed to take the high ground and his men suffered greatly from well-placed enemy fire. Laurens himself was wounded, and his second in command fell back to the main force at the Tullifinny, where Moultrie was compelled to retreat towards Charleston.

Directions: Take Exit 28 off I-95, Hwy. 462, bear right at the end of the ramp, and turn right at the stop sign. Proceed 1 mile to the bridge over the Coosawhatchie River just past where 462 turns off to the left. The battle took place just north of the river.

Stono Ferry

Date: June 20, 1779
Location: Near Rantowles, Charleston County
Commanders: Gen. Benjamin Lincoln; Col. John Maitland
Casualties: American—34k, 113w; British—26k, 103w

Charleston finally fell to the British in May 1780 but that had not been their first attempt to take the city. They had failed in June 1776 at Fort Moultrie and three years after that, Maj. Gen. Augustine Prevost pushed north from Savannah and was met and repulsed by both William Moultrie and Benjamin Lincoln. The British were entrenched on the Stono River, west of Charleston. From here they were able to forage on the mainland and protect their escape route down the river and to the Atlantic Ocean, but by June, it was determined that the base should be abandoned. With only 500 troops under Col. John Maitland, American general Benjamin Lincoln decided the fortification was weak enough to attack.

Lincoln had 1,400 troops under his command but his men became bogged down in the marsh before they even reached the redoubts and abatis the British had constructed. Once contact was made, heavy firing went on for an hour, and after the American cavalry was halted by British bayonets and musket fire, Lincoln withdrew his men. Casualties on both sides were about equal—approximately 150 killed and wounded. Although the British technically won, they abandoned their fortifications here and had failed to achieve their primary goal—the capture of Charleston.

Directions: From Charleston, take Hwy. 17 south to the turnoff to Kiawah and Seabrook islands (Main Rd.). Proceed approximately 1 mile to Limestone Bridge (note Old Ferry Rd. on the left); cross the bridge and park at the boat landing on the left. The ferry was across the river.

Biggin Bridge

Date: April 14, 1780
Location: Moncks Corner, Berkeley County
Commanders: Gen. Isaac Huger, Col. William Washington;
   Col. Banastre Tarleton
Casualties: American—14k, 19w, 64c; British—3w

Biggin Bridge. The ruins of Biggin Church, torched by the British during the war, still stand.

With Charleston under siege by the British, a supply line and possible escape route was being kept open by Gen. Isaac Huger and Col. William Washington (a cousin to George) at Biggin Bridge, near Moncks Corner, approximately 30 miles northwest of Charleston. To counter this effort, Sir Henry Clinton ordered a raiding party of Lt. Col. James Webster's

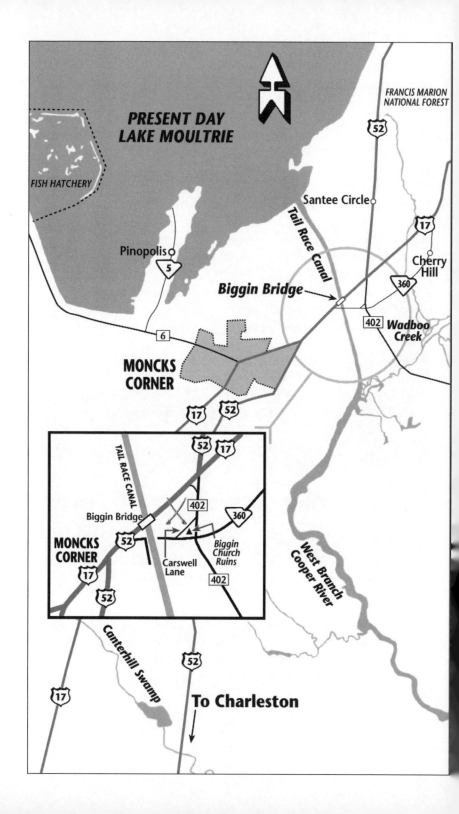

infantry and Col. Banastre Tarleton's cavalry to move from Quarter House, a well-known tavern and British stronghold on the outskirts of Charleston. The British advance reached the bridge, fortified by sleeping Americans, at 3 a.m. Huger's men immediately fell back towards their camp, with the British in murderous pursuit. American losses were relatively heavy—in terms of both men and supplies. Although Huger and Washington managed to escape, approximately 100 men were lost, and 50 wagonloads of supplies and ammunition and 400 horses were captured by Tarleton.[1]

The British remained in control of the Moncks Corner area for over a year. By July 1781, Biggin Church was being used as a supply depot. When Gen. Thomas Sumter moved against the forces here, Lt. Col. John Coates torched the church and fell back towards Charleston (see Quinby Bridge).

Directions: From Moncks Corner, take Hwy. 52 over the Tail Race Canal Bridge (Biggin Bridge). Turn right at the light—SR 402— which turns right; proceed about a mile and bear right onto Carswell Lane. The Biggin Church ruins are between these two roads.

Lenud's Ferry

Date: May 6, 1780
Location: Jamestown, Berkeley County
Commanders: Col. Anthony Walters White; Col. Banastre
    Tarleton
Casualties: Amerian—11k, 30w, 67c; British—2k

Lenud's Ferry. The original ferry landing can be seen between the present-day bridge and the railroad bridge.

By the spring of 1780, the British were on the verge of taking complete control of the lowcountry. Charleston was under siege and British foraging and raiding parties were active as far north as the Santee River.[1] North of the Santee, Patriots were gathering to meet these threats. Col. Anthony Walters White was in command of one of these units comprised of about 300 men, some of whom had seen action at Biggin Bridge. On the morning of May 6, White and his men captured a British detachment of foragers by crossing the river. He then marched downstream to recross at Lenud's Ferry with his prisoners in tow.

Unfortunately, Banastre Tarleton was in the area and had been tipped off to the Americans' exploits by a Loyalist informant. He managed to push forward at a rapid pace, reaching the ferry at 3 p.m. His 150 dragoons immediately charged the unsuspecting Americans. The rout was swift and complete. The British recaptured their foragers as well as 67 of the Americans, plus arms and horses. Many of the Americans who escaped, including White, did so by swimming across the river. The British lost only two killed.

Directions: From Moncks Corner, take Hwy. 17A to Jamestown. Turn left onto 17A/41. The highway marker is 0.7 mile on the right. Proceed another 0.5 mile and turn left onto a paved road, which leads to the boat landing. Walk under the bridge over the Santee River towards the old railroad bridge and you will see the old ferry landing.

Morris Ford

Date: May 1780
Location: Barnwell, Barnwell County
Commanders: Unknown
Casualties: Unknown

Morris Ford. The grave of John Mumford, killed in the battle, sits at the foot of the earthworks erected here.

According to memoirs of Tarleton Brown of Barnwell County, Loyalists under Benjamin John erected the earthworks here to protect the ford over the Salkehatchie River. In May 1780, just after Charleston fell to the British, Capt. John Mumford of the South Carolina militia was killed in the fighting that took place here while his unit was attempting to join Patriot forces in the vicinity.

Directions: From Barnwell, go south on Hwy. 278 for 2.5 miles. Cross the Salkehatchie River, then take a sharp left onto SR 70. The highway marker is a few hundred yards on the right. Colonel Mumford's grave is here and the earthworks are still intact. (Please help preserve them by not climbing them!)

Buford's Bloody Battleground

Date: May 29, 1780
Location: Near Lancaster, Lancaster County
Commanders: Col. Abraham Buford; Col. Banastre Tarleton
Casualties: American—113k, 150w, 53c; British—5k, 12w

Buford's Bloody Battleground. A simple monument stands at the foot of the mass grave of the Patriots killed here.

When Charleston fell to the British on May 12, 1780, after a six-week siege, there was but one remaining unit of Continental soldiers in the state—the Third Virginia Regiment commanded by Col. Abraham Buford, 350 strong and comprised in part by a detachment of Col. William Washington's cavalry. Buford had been sent to reinforce the city, but when news of the capitulation reached him at Jamestown on the Santee River, he had to beat a hasty retreat all the way back to North Carolina. Upon learning that Patriot governor John Rutledge was with Buford, Gen. Charles Cornwallis set out to capture the lot of them.[1] Realizing that he was 10 days behind them and he could not possibly catch up to Buford with his infantry, Cornwallis dispatched Col. Banastre Tarleton with 170 cavalry and 100 mounted infantry to continue the pursuit. With little rest in the oppressive heat, Tarleton pushed his dragoons 105 miles in 54 hours. He finally caught up with Buford on May 29 just short of the North Carolina line in what was then known as the Waxhaws settlement.

Fighting erupted immediately. Buford turned and formed his infantry into a single line for battle. They were only able to get off one volley before Tarleton's cavalry came charging through their ranks. The Patriots immediately recognized the suicidal futility of continued resistance and raised the white flag, but the British continued to attack. Dr. Robert Brownfield, a surgeon with Buford, described the ensuing slaughter: "The demand for quarters, seldom refused a vanquished foe, was at once found to be in vain; not a man was spared, and it was the concurrent testimony of all the survivors that for fifteen minutes after every man was prostrate they went over the ground plunging their bayonets into every one that exhibited any signs of life, and in some instances, where several had fallen over the others, these monsters were seen to throw off on the point of the bayonet the uppermost, to come at those beneath."

The murdering did not end until 113 Patriots were dead, 150 wounded (many of them mortally), and 53 captured. Buford escaped on horseback. British casualties were shamefully light—5 killed and 12 wounded.[2]

The Waxhaws Massacre, as the battle is sometimes called, left Southern Patriots seething over "Bloody Tarleton." Cries of "Buford's Quarter" or "Tarleton's Quarter" would often be repeated in fighting all over the South. Although the actions of the British can never be excused, Buford himself must shoulder some of the responsibility for the fate of his troops. While he may not have been able to choose his battleground, forming his men into a single line in the face of cavalry, and ordering them to hold their fire until the enemy was but 50 paces away, proved to be fatal mistakes for his men, many of whom are buried in a mass grave on the battlefield. Tarleton had achieved his objective, but he left South Carolina Patriots hungry for revenge.

Directions: Take Hwy. 9 east from Lancaster and go 9 miles to the intersection of SR 522. The battlefield is close to the southwest corner of the intersection.

Beckhamville

Date: June 6, 1780
Location: Near Great Falls, Chester County
Commanders: Capt. John McClure; Col. Housman[1]
Casualties: Unknown

Beckhamville. This battle took place in Alexander's Old Field.

Although the last of the Continental troops in South Carolina were defeated at Buford's Bloody Battleground, resistance to the British was far from over. Local militia, guerilla forces, and bands of friends and neighbors continued the fight for independence. The Battle of Beckhamville exemplifies this last group. Incensed by the news of Tarleton's massacre, Justice John

Gaston, an elderly and distinguished Patriot, gathered his nine sons, several nephews, and many of their friends together to counteract the efforts of the British, who had summoned the people to gather at Alexander's Old Field to pledge their loyalty to the king. Under the command of Justice Gaston's nephew Capt. John McClure, 32 men quietly made their way to the field, surrounded the Loyalists, and easily defeated them though they were 200 strong. The British were able to maintain an outpost at nearby Rocky Mount, but their efforts to enlist local Loyalists brought only limited success.

Directions: Take Hwy. 21 south from Fort Lawn and bear right on SR 97 just north of Great Falls. At the intersection, bear right to stay on 97 north. The granite marker and field are on the right just before SR 99 comes in from the right.

Williamson's Plantation/ Huck's Defeat

Date: July 12, 1780
Location: Brattonsville, York County
Commanders: Col. William Bratton, Capt. John McClure;
Capt. Christian Huck
Casualties: American—1k, 1w; British—36k, 29c

The Bratton house at Historic Brattonsville. William Bratton defeated British forces at nearby Williamson's Plantation.

Although the British now solidified their presence in South Carolina with outposts all along the midlands, partisan leaders managed to keep up a constant harassment. Thomas Sumter was knocking at the back door of the British stronghold at Rocky Mount and, in response, the commander there sent

41

Capt. Christian Huck of Tarleton's Legion to deal with the Patriots. Huck ravaged the countryside on his way to Hill's Iron Works, where he destroyed this valuable source of munitions and farm implements. Col. William Hill joined with Capt. John McClure, Col. William Bratton (who had defeated a band of Tories at Mobley's Meeting House), and Capt. Edward Lacey to engage Captain Huck, who would be camped at Williamson's Plantation.

On his way to Williamson's, Huck and his officers had struck terror in the hearts of local residents. At Captain McClure's house, Huck found two young men melting pewter dishes to make bullets for the Patriot cause. Huck dumped the boys in a corncrib and told them they would be hanged the next morning. When Mrs. McClure protested, he struck her with his sword and they rode off to Colonel Bratton's house. There, Mrs. Bratton was ordered to prepare a meal for the intruders, and when Huck demanded she tell him where her husband was, she professed ignorance. One of the officers snatched a reaping hook from the wall and held it to her throat, threatening to cut off her head if she did not disclose the whereabouts of the Patriots. She steadfastly refused and another officer intervened on her behalf before her blood was shed. Capt. Edward Lacey's home was also in the area, but his worry was not of his wife or mother covering for him and thus invoking Huck's wrath, but rather of his father betraying him, as the old man was an avowed Loyalist. Lacey had to tie him to his bed to keep him from warning Huck of the Patriots' movements.

Secure in the delusion that he commanded the area, Huck had failed to post pickets at his camp, which lay between rail fences lining the road. They never heard the Patriots who snuck up on the sleeping British and opened fire at 75 paces. Huck mounted his horse to rally his troops but was shot in the neck and killed. Few others escaped death or capture. This American victory is significant because it was the first time a loose-knit band of Patriots had met and conquered an organized unit of British regulars.

Directions: From York, take Hwy. 321 for 6 miles, turn left onto SR 165, and go 3 miles to Brattonsville. The granite marker is on the left and the actual battle site is 1.5 miles northeast of Historic Brattonsville.

Hill's Iron Works: From York, take Hwy. 161 east for approximately 8 miles and turn left onto Hwy. 274. Proceed approximately 4 miles to the granite marker on the right, which is 0.5 mile past the intersection of SR 1081 and just before the bridge over Allison Creek.

Gowen's Old Fort

Date: July 13, 1780
Location: Near Gowensville, Spartanburg County
Commanders: Colonels John Jones, John Thomas, Charles
  McDowell
Casualties: British—1k, 3w, 30c

In 1780, civil war was rampant in the upcountry between
Loyalist and Patriot Americans. A group of the former who
were pursuing Patriot colonel John Thomas camped for the
night at Gowen's Old Fort. Thomas was on his way to join Col.
Charles McDowell, who was trying to gather an army near the
North Carolina line. Another Patriot band, made up of 22
Georgia militia under Col. John Jones and also on their way to
join McDowell, fell upon the British here and surrounded and
attacked them. They killed one, wounded three, and captured
the remaining 30.

Another incident took place here in November 1781 that was
very similar to what happened at Lyndley's Fort in 1776. A group
of Loyalists under William ("Bloody") Bates,[1] made up of
Cherokees and white men dressed as Indians, attacked the fort
where local settlers had taken refuge. The fort surrendered due
to lack of ammunition, and when Bates' men entered, they massacred almost all the men, women, and children. Maj. John
Gowen, who was in command, was taken off to be burned at the
stake but later rescued when another band of Patriots overtook
and defeated Bates.

*Directions: From Campobello, go west on Hwy. 11, turn right onto
SR 184, and go 1.2 miles to the bridge over the South Pacolet River.
The fort was on the left.*

44

Fort Prince/McDowell's Camp

Date: July 15, 1780
Location: Near Wellford, Spartanburg County
Commanders: Colonels John Jones and Charles McDowell,
    Capt. Edward Hampton; Col. Alexander Innes, Maj. James
    Dunlap
Casualties: Amerian—10k, 20w; British—8k

*Fort Prince/McDowell's Camp. The monument commemorating this battle blends
into the grove of trees.*

Built in 1756, Fort Prince had served the early frontier settlers
as a refuge in times of Indian uprisings. It was occupied early in
the war by the Patriots but later taken by the British, who occupied it in 1780. From this base, Col. Alexander Innes sent out a
raiding party under Maj. James Dunlap, who encountered
Americans in the area, most of whom were gathering to join

forces with Col. Charles McDowell. They clashed at Gowen's Old Fort and Earles Ford, and on July 15, McDowell sent Capt. Edward Hampton and 52 men mounted on the best horses in camp in pursuit of Dunlap. Although the British were overtaken and forced to make a stand, the running fight ended when the British reached the safety of the fort.

Directions: From Spartanburg, go west on I-85 and take Exit 68, Hwy. 129, to Wellford. Take the first right onto Ft. Prince Rd. and drive 0.65 mile. The brown granite marker is in a clearing on the right among several tall oak trees, just past the house at 350 Ft. Prince Rd.

Hunt's Bluff

Date: August 1, 1780
Location: Near Blenheim, Marlboro County
Commanders: Maj. Tristram Thomas; Col. Archibald
  McArthur, Lieutenant Nairne
Casualties: Unknown

After a resounding victory at Saratoga and a new appointment as commander in chief of the Southern Department, Gen. Horatio Gates prepared to move from North Carolina towards the British stronghold at Camden. Many of the British outposts had to be abandoned to fortify Cornwallis at Camden, and in one of the early efforts of this objective, 100 sick and wounded soldiers lying in a makeshift hospital at the Old Parish Church of St. David's in Cheraw were evacuated. The flotilla of flatboats, under the command of Lieutenant Nairne with a Loyalist escort commanded by Col. William Henry Mills, headed down the Pee Dee River towards Georgetown. Mills was a physician who had begun the war as a Patriot but had switched sides according to the fortunes of conflict.

Patriot militia forces had gotten wind of the plans. Under the leadership of Maj. Tristram Thomas, they stationed themselves on a bluff at a sharp bend in the river with a commanding view in both directions. Thomas's men were armed only with their muskets, so he had them make "dummy" cannons. They chopped down trees, removed the branches, and positioned the trunks on the bluff. This trick had been used before and it would take a good measure of luck to pull off the ruse.

When the enemy boats came into sight, Thomas ordered his men to prepare the "guns" for firing and demanded immediate surrender. The British did so at once. Some reports claim that the Loyalist escort may have mutinied and turned over the boats and prisoners, perhaps as part of a prearranged plan. About 100 men surrendered, but a supply boat was also part of the flotilla and provided some much-needed military gear for the Patriot cause.

47

Directions: Take Hwy. 38 into Blenheim. Go west onto SR 57, Hunt's Bluff Rd. (which is SR 381 east of 38). The highway marker is approximately 4.5 miles ahead just after the road turns sharply to the right. At the turn, proceed straight ahead along the dirt road to the bluff.

Rocky Mount

Date: August 1, 1780
Location: Near Great Falls, Fairfield County
Commanders: Gen. Thomas Sumter; Lt. Col. George
  Turnbull
Casualties: American—6k, 8w; British—unknown

Rocky Mount.

With the British fortifying Camden, partisan activity under Thomas Sumter intensified. He hoped to take the British outpost at Rocky Mount with his 600 men—a reasonable objective, since the post was held by only 150 British regulars and consisted of two log houses and another frame building that was of "flimsy construction," according to Sumter's informants.

49

Sumter of course demanded surrender, but the post's commander, Col. George Turnbull, refused.

The ensuing battle lasted eight hours and was marked by repeated unsuccessful attempts by the Patriots to either penetrate the abatis or destroy the building with rifle fire, since Sumter had no artillery. This proved impossible, as the British had built a wall inside the exterior clapboard siding. Their last hope was to have two men cross over open ground under cover fire from their comrades, hide behind a large rock near the buildings, and try to set them on fire to smoke out the enemy.

The plan worked, despite a severe wound suffered by one of the volunteers. Unfortunately, just as the first roof ignited, a heavy rainstorm struck and extinguished the flames. Sumter was forced to retreat, and during this movement he met up with two parties of British reinforcements. In partial retribution, he was able to inflict more casualties on the enemy than his forces themselves suffered.

Directions: From Great Falls, go south on Hwy. 21 for approximately 4 miles and turn left onto SR 20. Proceed 2.4 miles to the granite marker on the right.

Hanging Rock

Date: August 1 and 6, 1780
Location: Near Heath Springs, Lancaster County
Commanders: Gen. Thomas Sumter; Maj. John Carden
Casualties: American—12k, 41w; British—200k & w

Hanging Rock. British Loyalists camped under this rock the night before the battle.

At the same time that Sumter was executing his attack on Rocky Mount, Maj. William Richardson Davie, with his force of less than 100 mounted infantry and dragoons, planned a simultaneous assault on another British outpost at Hanging Rock, about 15 miles east of Rocky Mount. His force was too small for a full-scale movement against the 500 Loyalists at the

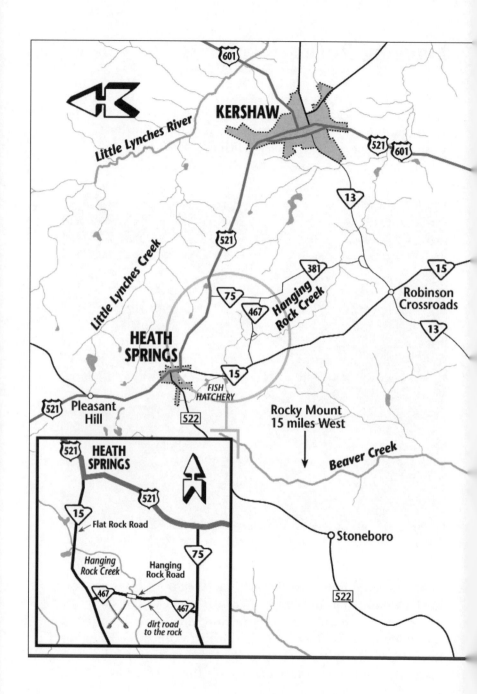

post, but he found three companies of Col. Samuel Bryan's North Carolina Loyalists camped at a farmhouse some distance from, but in full view of, the main camp. Taking advantage of the fact that neither Patriot nor Loyalist militia had uniforms but were clothed in the usual attire of common farmers (which they were), Davie sent half his men past the sentries and the house. They were not stopped or even questioned. The other half were waiting for their comrades to open fire, and when they did, the Loyalists were caught in the crossfire. Not a single Patriot was lost, but few of the enemy escaped death, wounding, or capture. Davie retreated with prisoners and supplies before the main force could organize and attack.

By this time, Sumter was moving to join Davie. Together their forces numbered about 800—more than enough to justify an assault on the British post at Hanging Rock, which was under the command of Maj. John Carden. Although Sumter and Davie had agreed on a strategy, the men became confused and all units attacked the British left, which soon broke and fled to the center, with the Americans following closely behind. The British rallied but were unable to withstand the deadly fire. Not a single British officer was left standing when the Patriots began to plunder their camp. The store of liquor was quickly located and the thirsty men could not resist. Many became inebriated despite Sumter's rebukes and orders to return to duty. In the face of this disorder, a detachment of British cavalry seized the opportunity and charged. Fortunately, Davie's dragoons, still sober, were able to rout them. The British, all of whom were American Loyalists, had lost 200 killed and wounded while the American casualties numbered only 12 killed and 41 wounded.

One of Davie's command was a 13-year-old local boy who served as a messenger, since he was a good rider and was familiar with the area. Young Andrew Jackson would grow up to become the seventh president of the United States.

Directions: From Heath Springs, go south on Hwy. 15 about 2 miles and turn left onto SR 467 (Hanging Rock Rd.). Go 0.8 mile to a dirt road that turns sharply to the right. This road is closed off but a short walk will take you to a path into the woods. Walk straight ahead to the rock. Hanging Rock Creek is below the rock. The battle took place on the other side of the creek between the water and Hwy. 15. A highway marker to the battle is in Heath Springs at the intersection of Hwy. 521 and 15.

Camden

Date: August 16, 1780
Location: Camden, Kershaw County
Commanders: Generals Horatio Gates, Baron deKalb;
  Generals Charles Cornwallis, Francis Rawdon
Casualties: American—250k, 800w; British—324k & w

Camden. The monument on the left marks the spot where Baron deKalb was mortally wounded.

After the fall of Charleston, the British were firmly in control of both Georgia and South Carolina. Cornwallis now set his sights on North Carolina, particularly after he learned that the newly appointed commander in chief of the Southern Department, Gen. Horatio Gates, had assembled the remnants of the American army there and was preparing to march south to the British outpost at Camden. Cornwallis immediately dropped his administrative duties in Charleston and headed for Camden, which was fortified with approximately 2,200 Redcoats under the command of Lord Francis Rawdon. Meanwhile, Gates assembled his army, the core of which he found in Hillsboro, North Carolina under the able leadership of Baron deKalb. They marched south, finally setting up camp at Rugeley's Mill, about 15 miles northwest of Camden. By then, the ranks had swelled to 4,000—many of them poorly trained militiamen who had never before seen battle.

Cornwallis was aware that he was badly outnumbered but knew he had no choice but to go to Gates and fight. Meanwhile, Gates prepared to continue on to Camden. By coincidence, both commanders decided on a night march along the same road at the same time. The two armies clashed eight miles north of Camden at 2 a.m. on the Waxhaws Road. Both fell back to regroup, form their battle lines, and wait for dawn. By one of those odd quirks of history, the physical condition of the Americans that night would play a significant role in the next day's fighting. The men had been issued a ration of beef and cornmeal, but due to a lack of supplies, the usual ration of "spirits" for men on the eve of battle was unavailable, and Gates ordered that molasses be issued as a substitute. Together with undercooked bread and meat, it had a debilitating effect on the men's digestive tracts. By morning, a good part of the army was sick with nausea, vomiting, and diarrhea. They were in no shape to fight, and when the Redcoats opened fire, panic spread throughout the ranks and the inexperienced and ill troops threw down their arms and fled.

The battle lasted about an hour. Only deKalb's Delaware and Maryland Continentals held fast. Baron deKalb himself was wounded 11 times but refused to leave the field.[1] To finish off the Americans, Cornwallis ordered Banastre Tarleton to take their rear. With British both in front and behind them, nearly all the Americans were either killed, wounded, or captured.[2] Horatio Gates, however, escaped. First he fled to Rugeley's Mill, where he hoped to rally his troops. Apparently unable to do so, he next went to Charlotte; three and one-half days and 180 miles later, he made it back to Hillsboro. Never before had an American general run so far, so fast. His contemporaries were more understanding of his actions than historians have been in explaining his seemingly inexcusable flight after such an ignominious failure. The British casualties numbered only about 300 killed and wounded.

After the battle, Cornwallis ordered the town fortified with breastworks, redoubts, and a stockade. Remnants of each can be seen today, along with the foundation of a powder magazine built by townsfolk in 1777 as a defense against the British, as well as the Kershaw-Cornwallis House, which the British commander used as his headquarters. All are part of Historic Camden, a reconstruction of the Revolutionary-era village.

Directions: Take Hwy. 521 north from Camden for approximately 6 miles. Bear left onto SR 58 (Flat Rock Rd.). The battlefield is 2.1 miles ahead on the right.

Musgrove's Mill

Date: August 18, 1780
Location: Near Cross Anchor, Spartanburg County
Commanders: Colonels Elijah Clarke, Isaac Shelby; Col.
  Alexander Innes, Maj. Patrick Ferguson
Casualties: American—4k, 7w; British—150k & w

Musgrove's Mill. The Musgrove property as it is seen from the Enoree River.

While the Americans were suffering a devastating defeat at Camden, another Patriot force was gathering and preparing for an attack on another British outpost. Militia units from South Carolina, North Carolina, and Georgia under colonels James Williams, Isaac Shelby, and Elijah Clarke, respectively, set out for Edward Musgrove's house and mill on the Enoree

Horseshoe Falls. This is where the Patriots camped the night before the battle.

River. Bad news awaited their arrival—the post had been reinforced the day before and now the Americans were outnumbered two to one. They camped near Horseshoe Falls on Cedar
Shoals Creek (which feeds into the Enoree River) to rest their
horses after the nonstop, 40-mile, all-night journey and to dis-
cuss strategy. They were now committed to battle since their
presence had been detected by enemy sentries.

The plan was simple—lure the enemy into attacking a fortified position. What is amazing is that the British fell for the old
trick. It worked beautifully. Capt. Shadrack Inman of the
Georgia militia led 25 men across the river and, feigning surprise
and retreat, drew the enemy back across the ford and into a
semicircular line of breastworks fortified by logs and brush that
the Patriots had hastily thrown up on a ridge just over the river.

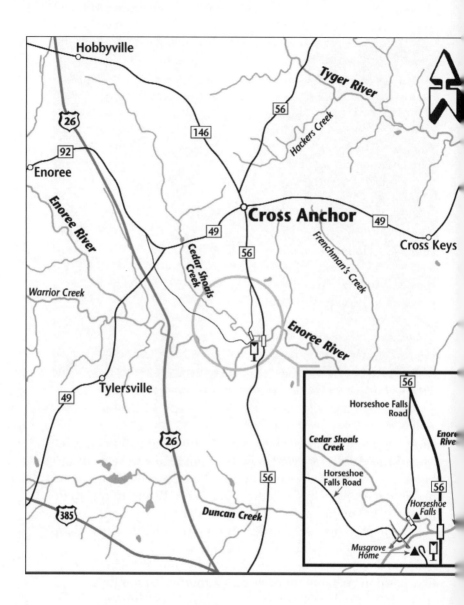

Fighting was fast and furious. The British line reeled under the initial volley, but the well-trained and experienced Redcoats were able to inflict as much damage as they had taken, particularly with their reinforcements and superior numbers. The tide of battle turned several times before it was over and the British retreated back across the river, leaving nearly half their force either killed, wounded, or captured. The Patriots had lost only four killed and seven wounded. One of them was the courageous Captain Inman, who was shot seven times, once in the head, and who is buried on the field.

Elated with their victory, the Patriots hoped to push on to Ninety Six. But in the aftermath of battle, they learned of the American defeat at Camden and were forced to move north into North Carolina. Shelby and Clarke would soon meet again one of the British commanders, Maj. Patrick Ferguson, at a place called Kings Mountain.

Directions: From Cross Anchor, take Hwy. 56 south. Proceed approximately 1.8 miles from the intersection of Hwy. 56 and 49 and bear right onto Horseshoe Falls Rd. Cross over the one-lane bridge at the bottom of the hill and park on the left. Follow the path to Horseshoe Falls, where the Patriots camped the night before the battle. Continue on the road 0.3 mile and park just ahead on the left, where the old bridge and ford were located and where the present-day canoe access is located. Musgrove's home was across the river. The battle took place on the ridge on the opposite side of the road. Go back to Hwy. 56 and turn right, heading south. Proceed 1.5 miles to the new bridge over the Enoree River. On the other side of the bridge on the right is the granite marker commemorating the battle.

Black Mingo Creek

Date: September 28, 1780
Location: Near Rhems, Georgetown County
Commanders: Gen. Francis Marion; Col. John Coming Ball
Casualties: American—2k, 8w; British—3k, 1w, 13c

The port of Georgetown was under the control of the British and from there, they supplied numerous outposts. One of the closer outposts was at Patrick Dollard's Red House Tavern at Shepherd's Ferry over Black Mingo Creek. But this was Francis Marion's country and many of his men lived in the area. They all heartily agreed that it was time to oust the British from their territory. The post was commanded by a local Loyalist rice king, Col. John Coming Ball, who held tight control of the ferry. Naturally, he would not allow the Patriots passage. Marion planned a night attack. He and his guerillas arrived at the Willtown Bridge (a short distance upstream) about midnight, but British sentries heard their horses' hooves on the wooden planks of the bridge and alerted the post.[1] Rather than hole his men up in the tavern, Ball dispersed them in a field to the west. They were waiting when Marion arrived. Buckling under heavy fire at first, the Americans managed to regroup and within 15 minutes had driven the British back into the swamp. Among the booty captured was Colonel Ball's horse, which was handed over to the Swamp Fox. General Marion renamed it "Ball" and rode it for the remainder of the war.

Directions: From Rhems, take Hwy. 41/51 north for approximately 2 miles to the bridge over Black Mingo Creek. Cross the bridge, turn right, and park at the boat landing. The tavern and ferry were about a mile upstream, now on private property.

Kings Mountain

Date: October 7, 1780
Location: Near Blacksburg, York County
Commanders: Colonels William Campbell, Isaac Shelby; Maj.
   Patrick Ferguson
Casualties: American—28k, 62w; British—225k, 160w, 700c

Kings Mountain. Memorial to Col. Patrick Ferguson, the only native Englishman on the field.

Following his resounding victory at Camden, Cornwallis boldly pushed north to establish an outpost at Charlotte, North Carolina, thus securing a large portion of the South for the Crown. Maj. Patrick Ferguson was left in command of the area of Ninety Six. A fiery Scotsman, Ferguson had invented the first breech-loading rifle. Despite its effective use at Brandywine in 1777, he was wounded in that battle, leaving him with the use of only one arm. His spirit was undaunted, however. With hundreds of American Loyalists under his command, Ferguson sent a message to frontiersmen who had begun to organize in resistance to the Crown: "If you do not desist from your opposition to the British arms and take protection under my standard, I will march my army over the mountains, hang your leaders, and lay your country waste with fire and sword." Equally determined, these "over-mountain men" only took on new vigor from the threat.

Originating from Sycamore Shoals on the Watauga River, in what is now northeastern Tennessee, the Patriot forces began to gather under Colonels Charles McDowell, John Sevier, Isaac Shelby and William Campbell. Simultaneously, Patriots were gathering in the Piedmont of the Carolinas in almost equal numbers. As the combined troops moved southwest, Ferguson learned of their advance and fell back with his force to Kings Mountain[1] to await the reinforcements he had requested from Cornwallis. Unfortunately for the Loyalists, those reinforcements never came.

On October 7, the over-mountain men quietly took their positions, practically surrounding the base of the mountain. The opening shots of the battle were fired around 3 p.m., when the Patriots were finally detected. Although it may seem that men fighting uphill would be easy targets for troops positioned along the crest of the mountain, in reality, the tendency is to overshoot, and that is precisely what happened. Ferguson then had his men fix their bayonets. Three times they charged and three times they were sent reeling back to their mountaintop position. In a final effort to rally his troops, Ferguson rode from one end of the line to the other, waving his sword in his one good hand and blowing a silver whistle. He was immediately shot down, and with one foot caught in his horse's stirrup, he was dragged a short distance before being propped against a tree. He died moments later of numerous gunshot wounds.[2] His second in command was forced to surrender.

Although Ferguson was an able and effective military commander, the responsibility for the defeat at Kings Mountain rests squarely on his shoulders. The strategic advantage of a position on the crest of a mountain was far outweighed by the background and skills of the Patriot forces. These frontiersmen were highly skilled Indian fighters. Their survival in the untamed wilderness depended on it. Excellent marksmen who were used to fighting from tree to tree and rock to rock, they were in their element at Kings Mountain. American colonel Henry Lee summarized Ferguson's position as "more assailable by the rifle than defensible with the bayonet." Moreover, Ferguson had failed to erect breastworks, although his troops took position in plenty of time to do so.[3]

What took place after the surrender is the object of much debate and disagreement. It is known that a number of prisoners were fired upon and killed, fighting briefly resumed, and it took commanders on both sides some time to restore order. There are reports that fresh troops on both sides arrived simultaneously and took up the fight, unaware that a surrender had taken place. Others claim that shouts of "Buford's Quarter" were heard as the prisoners were massacred. Whether from ignorance or revenge, the final shots put an ignominious end to the battle. After only one hour of combat, Ferguson had lost 225 killed, 160 wounded, and 700 captured[4] (his entire force), while the Patriot losses were only 28 killed and 62 wounded of their nearly 1,800 men engaged. This was truly civil war. Ferguson was the only British man on the field—all other combatants were Americans.

Ferguson's defeat and death at Kings Mountain would have a far-reaching effect on the British forces in the South. Cornwallis had to fall back once again, this time to Winnsboro. The British would never again gain and keep control of the area north and west of the line of bases through the midlands of South Carolina. Kings Mountain was the beginning of a lengthy retreat to Charleston.

Directions: From York, go 13 miles north on Hwy. 161 to the park entrance on the left, or take Exit 2 from I-85 in North Carolina.

Fishdam Ford

Date: November 9, 1780
Location: Near Carlisle, Chester County
Commanders: Gen. Thomas Sumter; Maj. James Wemyss
Casualties: American—4k, 10w; British—4k, 20w

With the victory at Kings Mountain, partisan recruits and activities were flourishing. In response, Cornwallis, who was now camped at Winnsboro, sent Banastre Tarleton after Marion and Maj. James Wemyss in search of Sumter.[1] Wemyss found the Gamecock camped on the east bank of the Broad River, about 30 miles northwest of Winnsboro, at Fishdam Ford, a chain of rocks erected by Cherokee Indians to trap fish in the shallow part of the river. He arrived at about 1 a.m. and, not willing to forfeit the element of surprise or risk detection, ordered an attack. Wemyss was shot by pickets almost immediately. His second in command was unsure of the plan and ordered the troops to advance. By now the Americans had gathered their arms and lay hiding in the woods behind trees. When the mounted British rode into the light of the sentries' campfires, they made easy targets. Although they subsequently dismounted to fight as infantry and managed a rally, they were badly outnumbered and easily beaten back.

In the meantime, Sumter himself was nearly captured when a Loyalist spy led the British to his tent. Just as two Redcoats came in the front, Sumter dashed out the back and jumped over a fence and through the underbrush to hide at the riverbank. Without their leaders, both sides retreated, but the Patriots did not go far and returned at dawn to take the field and tend the wounded.

When they arrived, they found Wemyss with a broken arm and a shattered knee but still alive. In his pocket, Sumter found a list of the men he had hanged and the homes and churches he had burned. Sumter read the list, crumpled it up, and tossed it into the fire. Though this was hailed by some as a humanitarian gesture, other historians feel that Sumter was considering the retribution of Cornwallis if the Patriots meted out the punishment Wemyss so justly deserved. As it was, Wemyss eventually recovered and would go on to fight again. So would Sumter.

Directions: From Carlisle, take Hwy. 121/72 east for several miles. Cross over the Broad River; on the other side of the bridge on the left is both the highway marker and the granite marker. The only nearby parking is a pull-off for the entrance to a quarry, about 100 feet east of the markers. The fishdam and the ford are a few hundred feet upstream.

Blackstock's Ford

Date: November 20, 1780
Location: Near Cross Keys, Union County
Commanders: Gen. Thomas Sumter; Col. Banastre Tarleton
Casualties: American—3k, 4w; British—92k, 75w

Blackstock's Ford. The monument among these trees overlooks the ford over the Tyger River.

With Patriot victories at Kings Mountain and Fishdam Ford, Sumter's troops now numbered about 1,000 and the Gamecock was ready to move against Ninety Six. In the meantime, Cornwallis called off Tarleton's fruitless pursuit of Francis Marion and sent him chasing after Sumter. With warning from a British deserter, Sumter instead turned west and was preparing to ford the Tyger River near Blackstock's Plantation. Knowing he would have to run to catch Sumter, Tarleton left his infantry and artillery behind and continued on with his cavalry. Sumter was ready for him. He posted his men behind the fence along the road to the ford as well as in the Blackstocks' farmhouse and outbuildings. Realizing he was badly outnumbered and outpositioned, Tarleton attempted to delay in order to wait for the rest of his troops and his artillery. But Sumter was well aware of his advantage and sent his men forward to initiate the battle.[1] Unfortunately, the men fired at too great a distance and were charged by British bayonets before they could reload. But Hampton's sharpshooters, safely ensconced in the outbuildings, effectively reduced the force before they could inflict much damage.

The British line broke and fell into a retreat. They had lost 92 killed and 75 wounded. Sumter rode forward to solidify his victory when a British unit covering the retreat saw him and fired. Sumter was wounded in six places by buckshot but managed to ride back to the command post. He was tended by a surgeon at the Blackstock house and then carried off to the mountains on a bull's hide attached to poles and slung between two horses, to recover. He would be out of action for the next two months.

Unwilling to admit defeat, the pompous Tarleton claimed victory. After all, he had prevented an attack on Ninety Six and Sumter's troops had dispersed after crossing the river. However, partisan forces nearly always dispersed after battle to re-form when needed, and the boost in Patriot morale left no doubt as to who were the true victors. Patriot casualties were only three killed and four wounded.

Directions: From Cross Anchor, take Hwy. 49 east into Union County; proceed approximately 1 mile and turn left onto SR 51 (Blackstock Rd.) at the highway marker. Bear right at the sign onto Monument Rd., then left at the fork. The granite marker is 1.3 miles ahead. As of the date of publication, the bronze plaque on the marker was missing. The Tyger River and the ford where the battle took place are at the bottom of the hill.

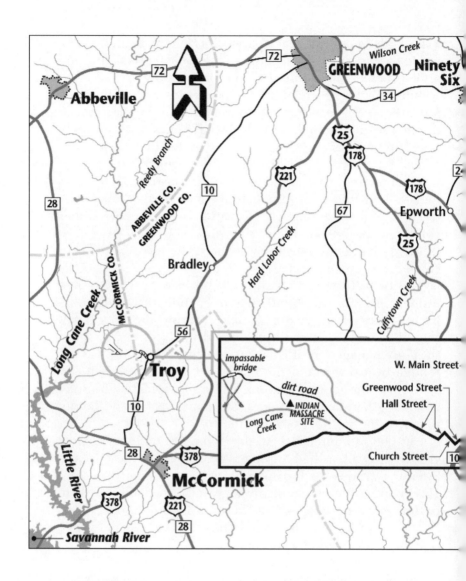

Long Cane

Date: December 12, 1780
Location: Near Troy, McCormick County
Commanders: Colonels Elijah Clarke, James McCall; Col.
  John H. Cruger
Casualties: American—14k, 7w; British—unknown

Long Cane. A simple granite marker is placed at the mass grave of the colonial settlers massacred at this battle site.

The British stronghold at Ninety Six was the only post that had remained unmolested by the Patriots. The commander there, Col. John H. Cruger, learned that some of Sumter's officers who were with him at Blackstock's Ford were preparing to move against the fortification. Colonels Elijah Clarke and James McCall joined up with Col. Benjamin Few of Georgia and marched towards the Long Cane settlement (about 30 miles southwest of Ninety Six), where they hoped to arouse the Patriot sentiments of the populace and gain some new recruits to the cause. The settlement had been the victim of a Cherokee Indian attack in which 150 settlers were murdered.

To counter the Patriots' move, Colonel Cruger sent Col. Isaac Allen with about 450 Redcoats and Loyalists towards the American camp. Colonel Few, with about the same number, sent out an advance force of about 100 to meet the enemy. Initially the British were repulsed but although the main body of Patriots was in reserve, both Clarke and McCall were wounded early in the battle and the American forces fled in confusion. The British dragoons charged, inflicting deadly blows as they advanced.[1] Colonel Few failed to bring up the main body and instead ordered a full retreat.

Directions: From McCormick, take Hwy. 28 north. Bear right onto Hwy. 10 into Troy. Turn left onto SR 24 (W. Main St.), following signs to Indian Massacre Grave (left on Greenwood St., right on Church St., left on Hall Rd.). You will reenter McCormick County. The pavement ends at the fork; bear right and go 1.5 miles to the massacre site on the left. Go back to where you last turned; turn left and follow the road 0.7 mile to the bridge, which is impassable. The battle took place in this area.

Halfway Swamp

Date: December 12, 1780
Location: Near Rimini, Clarendon County
Commanders: Gen. Francis Marion; Maj. Robert McLeroth
Casualties: American—6w; British—6k & w

Halfway Swamp, one of South Carolina's beautiful cypress swamps.

When Francis Marion learned that a detachment of
Redcoats under the command of Maj. Robert McLeroth was
moving from Charleston towards Cornwallis's headquarters at
Winnsboro, he wasted no time gathering his force together to
stop them. He caught up with their rear guard at Halfway
Swamp and killed a few of their pickets in what he thought

Halfway Swamp Mill. An old mill can be explored here.

would be the opening shots of the battle. McLeroth, however, fled another mile and a half north to an open field to get his troops into position, and when Marion's army arrived, he sent a messenger under a flag of truce to the Swamp Fox. He accused Marion of violating the rules of warfare by shooting his pickets and challenged him to a duel between 20 selected men on each side. Marion replied that he would stop shooting armed pickets when the British stopped burning the homes of innocent civilians and quickly accepted the challenge. Not one man refused Marion's request. The 20 boldly marched out to meet an equal number of Redcoats, but when the troops got within 100 yards of one another, the British turned around and marched back to their lines. Marion's men celebrated their victory, but under the cover of darkness, McLeroth slipped away and headed for Singleton's Mill, 10 miles to the north. Marion sent a detachment ahead to beat them there but, finding the Singleton family ill with smallpox, the Patriots refused to occupy the buildings and the British continued on their way unmolested.

Directions: From Rimini, take Hwy. 76 south for 1.2 miles to the bridge and swamp. The open field where the duel took place is on private property in Rimini in Sumter County just north of the railroad tracks.

Cowpens

Date: January 17, 1781
Location: Near Cowpens, Cherokee County
Commanders: Gen. Daniel Morgan; Col. Banastre Tarleton
Casualties: American—12k, 60w; British—110k, 200w, 527c

Cowpens.

There is much debate over whether Kings Mountain or Cowpens marked the turning point of the American Revolution. After Kings Mountain, the British finally realized that they could not depend on Loyalist sentiment and support to secure the South. At Cowpens, American general Daniel Morgan displayed his brilliance in military strategy

and forced the British to the realization that Tarleton's celebrated legion was not invincible. Tarleton had been defeated
at Blackstock's but Cornwallis still had confidence in him.
When the British commander heard that Gen. Nathanael
Greene had split his army at Charlotte and had taken 1,000
men east towards Cheraw and sent 600 west under Morgan,
Cornwallis sent Tarleton after Morgan.[1]

With his forces augmented by Andrew Pickens and his
troops, Morgan kept his army moving and tried to keep clear
of Tarleton. But Morgan was a fighter, not a runner, and decided to stop and make a stand. He camped about eight miles
north of Cowpens, so named for the cattle herds that were win-
tered here. The British were not far behind, and just before 7
a.m. their advance party of scouts met up with and were turned
back by Morgan's forward line.

General Morgan's plan was ingenious. He formed his army
into three lines. The forward line was made up of approximately 150 riflemen who hid in the bushes and behind trees.
It was these men that Tarleton's troops first encountered, thus
preventing them from discovering the positions of the main
body of Americans. The forward line was to fire twice and fall
back to the second line. The middle line was made up of
Pickens' men. They had instructions to wait until the riflemen
fell back and then fire, especially at officers; "look for
epaulets," they were told. These troops were then to move
around the flanks and re-form behind the rear line of
Continentals under the command of Col. John E. Howard of
Maryland, who were stationed on one of the low ridges that
bordered the field. Lastly, Morgan held Col. William
Washington's cavalry in reserve.

Tarleton could not wait for battle to begin. With his advance
heading back, he formed his army into a single line, with cavalry and some infantry in reserve. He had two cannons on the
field with the harmless-sounding name of "grasshoppers," but
they produced a deadly fire. Morgan's forward riflemen had
done their job, but the second line broke after they returned the
initial volley of the British and then were charged with bayonets.

They had accomplished their goal, though—a majority of the British officers had been killed or wounded, and the militiamen retreated in an orderly fashion to the rear of the main line of Continentals.

The British line continued to advance despite a lack of leadership. Howard ordered his right flank to pivot so as to trap the British in a crossfire. In the confusion, the Patriots began to retreat. But seeing the mistake, Morgan allowed them to march back a short distance and then, with reinforcements from the advance lines, he had them turn and fire at the British, who were just tasting victory, and finally charge them with bayonets fixed. The British advance was finished off by Washington's cavalry charge.

For the first time in his career, Banastre Tarleton was unable to rally his men, who were now dropping their arms and calling for quarter. The American militiamen were anxious to give them "Tarleton's Quarter," but Morgan would not allow any wanton murder of prisoners to take place in his command. Finally, Tarleton managed to convince 40 dragoons who had not yet surrendered or fled to make one final charge with him. They were chased from the field by the cavalry, with Washington in the lead. The two great commanders came face to face. Washington crossed swords with another British officer and had his weapon broken off at the hilt. His young black body servant shot the Redcoat in the shoulder just before he swung his saber at Washington. Next, Tarleton fired at Washington. The bullet missed the colonel but wounded his horse, just before the remainder of the cavalry was finally able to clear the field of the enemy. The British left behind 110 dead and over 700 wounded and captured, while Morgan's forces only suffered 12 killed and 60 wounded. Among the captured supplies were 800 muskets and the two "grasshopper" cannons. The entire battle was over in less than an hour.

Directions: From Gaffney, take I-85 west to Exit 83, Hwy. 110 north. Go about 6 miles. Turn right onto SR 11; the park entrance is on the right.

Mount Hope Swamp

Date: March 9, 1781
Location: Near Greeleyville, Williamsburg County
Commanders: Gen. Francis Marion, Col. Peter Horry; Col. John Watson
Casualties: Unknown

Aware that the British, under Col. John Watson, were moving from Fort Watson to attack his camp at Snow's Island, Marion left a small detachment there to guard the base and moved out with most of his men towards the fort. Early in March the two forces met up at Wyboo Swamp, now under the waters of Lake Marion. A few days later, Marion attempted to prevent the British advance at Mount Hope Swamp. He had his men take up the planks of the bridge, and he posted a unit of riflemen under Col. Peter Horry to slow down the progress of the enemy. Watson was delayed several hours waiting for his artillery but was eventually able to break through.

Next, Watson moved towards Kingstree, but Marion engaged him once again at Lower Bridge over the Black River.[1] This time Watson's artillery was not as successful. Marion's men destroyed the bridge and picked off the British as they made every possible effort to advance. They even made retrieval of the wounded difficult for the enemy. Watson's forces were slowly and systematically depleted as he retreated towards Georgetown, never able to reach his goal at Snow's Island.

Directions: From Greeleyville, take Hwy. 375 south from the intersection with Hwy. 521 for 2.5 miles. Turn right onto SR 148 (Lesesne Rd.), which ends at a dirt road. Turn right onto the dirt road (River Rd.) and drive 0.6 mile to a small bridge over Mount Hope Swamp. The bridge is just past St. John's Baptist Church.

Snow's Island

Date: Late March 1781
Location: Johnsonville, Florence County
Commanders: Col. Hugh Ervin; Col. Welbore Ellis Doyle
Casualties: American—7k, 15w

Named for onetime owners James and William Snow, this peninsula is bordered on the east, west, and north by the Pee Dee River and Clark's and Lynches creeks, respectively. Francis Marion used it as his base camp from the fall of 1780 to March 1781, when the British finally set out to destroy it and capture the Swamp Fox. British lord Francis Rawdon had given up trying to catch Sumter and instead devised a pincers movement in his quest for Marion. He sent Col. John Watson from Fort Watson on the Santee River towards the northeast of Snow's Island and Col. Welbore Ellis Doyle from Camden towards the southeast.

Having learned of these movements, Marion left a small detachment under Col. Hugh Ervin at the camp and took the bulk of his brigade out to skirmish with Watson for the next few weeks. They beat him all the way back to Georgetown. Meanwhile, Doyle reached Snow's Island and managed to kill, wound, or capture 22 of Marion's men before the others escaped. Ervin was able to throw the arms and ammunition into the river to prevent their capture by the British.

Directions: From Johnsonville, take Hwy. 41/51 north. Bear right onto Hwy. 41/378 into Marion County. Bear right onto Hwy. 378 and go 5.5 mi. to a pull-off on the right, just before you reach Hwy. 908. Turn right onto the first dirt road past the pull-off (Bluff Rd.) and proceed 1.7 miles to Dunham's Bluff. From here, Snow's Island can be seen across the Pee Dee River.

Waxhaws Church

Date: April 9, 1781
Location: Near Lancaster, Lancaster County
Commanders: None
Casualties: Unknown

Waxhaws Church. Pres. Andrew Jackson grew up nearby.

This little-documented skirmish may have only been a raiding party. About 150 Loyalists attacked the settlement, burned
several houses and this church, and killed, wounded, or captured a number of settlers, probably disbanded Patriot militia.
The church, like many others, was used as a hospital during
the war and is noteworthy because it was the first church in the

upcountry, having been established in 1755. Andrew Jackson's father is buried in the churchyard.

Directions: From Lancaster, take Hwy. 9 west. The church is on the right, 5 miles past the intersection with Hwy. 9 Bypass.

Fort Watson

Date: April 15-23, 1781
Location: Near Summerton, Clarendon County
Commanders: Gen. Francis Marion, Col. Henry Lee; Lt.
  James McKay
Casualties: American—2k, 6w; British—120c

Fort Watson. The fort was built atop this ancient Indian mound.

Named for its builder, Col. John Watson, this British outpost was constructed on top of an old Indian mound at Wright's Bluff on the Santee River.[1] Its location made it a major supply and communications link between Charleston and Camden and, therefore, a target for both Sumter and Marion. In late February, Sumter managed to capture 20 wagonloads of supplies intended for Lord Rawdon's army at the Battle of Manigault's Ferry. Sumter floated them down the Santee and was to meet the flotilla before it reached Wright's Bluff, but through the treachery of one of the pilots, the boats passed the meeting point and were recaptured by the British. Sumter tried to capture them back through a suicidal frontal assault on Fort Watson. The Gamecock was unaware that the fort had been reinforced just hours before by 400 infantry, and the Americans lost both men and horses.

Marion used different tactics in his attempt to take the fort two months later. Together with Col. Henry ("Lighthorse Harry") Lee, he lay siege to the post. Partisan bands traveled light and without the artillery necessary to barrage the fort, so Marion had to devise alternate methods of forcing a surrender. He first cut off their water supply, but the British simply dug a well. Starving the British out would take months. So Col. Hezekiah Maham, of Marion's brigade, came up with an idea. He took a number of men out into the woods to fell trees, remove their branches, and notch the ends as though they were going to build a log cabin—something most of them had experience with. During the night, they carried the logs next to the fort and constructed a square tower that rose to a height of 50 feet—10 feet higher than the fort walls. When dawn broke, riflemen standing on a platform in the tower rained a deadly fire into the fort. Its commander, Lt. James McKay, quickly surrendered. The device was so effective that Maham's Tower, as it was thereafter known, was used in other sieges in the Southern campaign. The victorious Americans captured over 100 British and their supplies and then destroyed the fort. Marion reported two killed and six wounded on his side in the siege. It was the first fort captured from the British. The war in the South would soon be over for them.

Directions: From Santee, take I-95 north over Lake Marion to Exit 102. Take Hwy. 15/301 north for 1 mile, turn left onto SR 803 (at the sign for Santee National Wildlife Refuge and Fort Watson), and go 1 mile to the fort, which was built atop a ceremonial Santee Indian mound.

Hobkirk's Hill

Date: April 25, 1781
Location: Near Camden, Kershaw County
Commanders: Gen. Nathanael Greene, Col. William
    Washington; Gen. Francis Rawdon
Casualties: American—18k, 108w; British—258k & w

Hobkirk's Hill.

For the British, the story of the American Revolution is one
of winning the battles but losing the war. Hobkirk's Hill exemplifies this adage. By the time the battle here took place,
Francis Marion had captured Fort Watson, the major supply
line between Charleston and Camden, and Lord Francis
Rawdon, commander at the Camden post, knew that it was

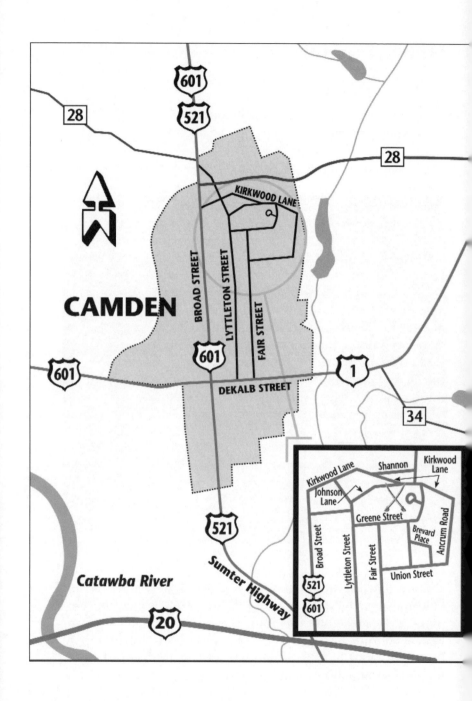

CAMDEN

Catawba River

Sumter Highway

Kirkwood Lane
Shannon
Kirkwood Lane
Johnson Lane
Greene Street
Brevard Place
Ancrum Road
Broad Street
Lyttleton Street
Fair Street
Union Street

only a matter of time before reinforcements would be reaching Gen. Nathanael Greene. Greene had settled down on Hobkirk's Hill, a low ridge about a mile and a half north of Camden. Rawdon was taking no chances. He had been informed that his forces not only outnumbered Greene's, but that the Americans were without their artillery. The British general ordered all but the sickest soldiers to gather arms for an assault on the American position.

Greene's troops were busy with morning camp chores when the advance pickets were engaged. They were more than ready for the British when they arrived; in fact they had a surprise for them—three field artillery pieces. Together, they had a devastating effect on the British. Making the most of his advantage, Greene ordered the center to advance and attempted to have his flanks turn the British line. But Rawdon's men recovered in time for the commander to extend his own line and check this movement. Then Rawdon fell into a bit of luck. A regiment of Maryland Continentals mistook an order to re-form for an order to withdraw. The American center began to collapse and the British were about to take the American flanks and capture the three cannons, when Col. William Washington's cavalry, who were attempting to take the British rear, returned just in time to save the artillery. Greene retreated to the area where the first battle of Camden took place, and Rawdon fell back to Camden. Only the dead and wounded occupied the field. Although he claimed victory, Rawdon was soon thereafter forced to abandon the post and retire towards Charleston. Greene moved in and destroyed the British fortifications.

Among the prisoners liberated by the Americans at Camden was 14-year-old Andrew Jackson, who had been incarcerated for attending a gathering of Patriots at Waxhaws Presbyterian Church. The high-spirited boy had good reason for hating the British. Not only had they ravaged the countryside around his home and thrown him into prison, but when he refused to polish the boots of a British officer, the officer struck the boy with his sword, leaving him with wounds on his hand and head. Jackson carried the scars for life.

Directions: From Camden, go north on Lyttleton Street, turn right onto Kirkwood Ln. (SR 28), which is 0.2 mile past the highway marker for Hobkirk's Hill. Kirkwood becomes a dirt road as it proceeds through Kirkwood Heights. The granite marker is 0.3 mile on the right. (Kirkwood Ln. can also be accessed from Broad St.—Hwy 521.)

Fort Motte

Date: May 12, 1781
Location: Near Fort Motte, Calhoun County
Commanders: Gen. Francis Marion, Col. Henry Lee;
  Lieutenant McPherson
Casualties: American—unknown; British—150c

Fort Motte. The Motte home was on a bluff overlooking the Congaree River.

Rebecca Brewton Motte had prominent Charleston family connections. Sister to Miles Brewton and widow of the long-serving provincial treasurer Jacob Motte, Rebecca nevertheless removed to her plantation on the Congaree River following the British occupation of Charleston.[1] The British soon took over that house and fortified it for use as an outpost along

89

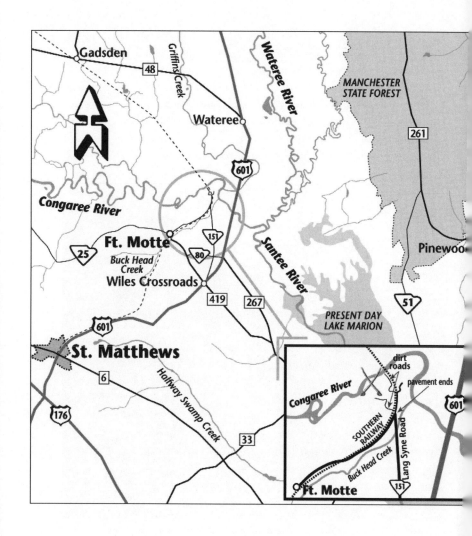

their supply line from Charleston, forcing Mrs. Motte to take up residence in the overseer's house.

It was May 1781 when Francis Marion and Lighthorse Harry Lee arrived after their success at Fort Watson, ready to mete out the same punishment to the British posted here at Fort Motte. As fate would have it, the fort had been recently reinforced (just like Fort Watson) and now held 150 men under

Lieutenant McPherson. Marion had one artillery piece with him and prepared to lay siege to the fort. He had his men dig trenches along a natural ravine in an effort to get as close as possible before launching an all-out assault. In the meantime, however, Lord Francis Rawdon was on his way from Camden, only 35 miles to the north, and Marion quickly realized that more expedient measures were called for. He decided to set the house on fire and, being a gentleman, consulted Mrs. Motte before taking action. She not only consented but provided Marion with the means necessary to put his plan to work. She gave him some "fire arrows" that ignited on impact, which her late husband had procured on his worldly travels. She may have also provided the bow with which to shoot them, although the Patriots could have quickly fashioned their own bow or even shot them from their muskets. Either way, the hot, dry, wood-shingle roof was soon set ablaze. The British tried to tear off the shingles but were discouraged by Marion's artillery fire, and Lieutenant McPherson was forced to surrender. Formalities of the capitulation were delayed while all available hands, British and American, worked to put out the fire in order to save at least part of Mrs. Motte's home. That evening, she served dinner to officers on both sides in the part of her house that had survived the fire.

Although Rawdon had seen the entire affair from across the river, Marion's forces prevented him from coming to the aid of his compatriots. He moved on toward Moncks Corner, while Marion continued his endeavor to capture the British outposts that dotted South Carolina's midlands.

Directions: From St. Matthews, take Hwy. 601 north. Just past the intersection with Hwy. 419 (approx. 7.5 miles), bear left onto SR 151 (Lang Syne Rd.) and continue 3 miles to the stop sign. The granite D.A.R. marker is straight ahead at the top of the hill in a clearing and enclosed within a small wooden fence. The site is on private property. Turn right onto the dirt road and proceed 0.5 mile to the railroad tracks. Cross the tracks and continue on another 0.3 mile beside the tracks to the railroad bridge over the Congaree River.

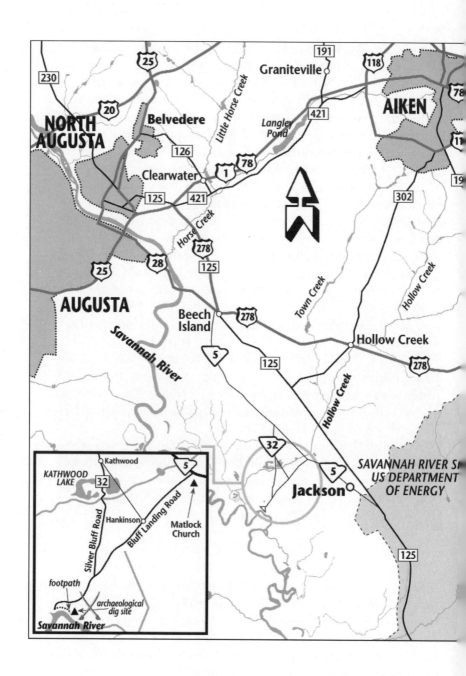

Fort Galphin

Date: May 21, 1781
Location: Near Jackson, Aiken County
Commanders: Col. Henry Lee, Maj. John Rudolph; Capt.
    Thomas Hanlocke
Casualties: American—1k, 8w; British—4k

Fort Galphin. Access to the Savannah River was vital to this plantation.

Known as Fort Dreadnought by the British and situated on
Silver Bluff on the Savannah River, this was the home of
George Galphin, an Indian trader and ardent Patriot who had
built the home in 1750 and used it as a trading post. Located
10 miles downriver from Augusta, the fort had great strategic
importance and changed hands several times during the war.

In May 1781, the British were in control, with Capt. Thomas Hanlocke in command. Although trade with the Indians had ceased years before, the British still gave presents to the local tribes in order to buy their loyalty. The annual Indian gifts had just been stockpiled in Fort Galphin when Col. Lighthorse Harry Lee made his move against the post. Not only was he after the much-needed supplies (including guns and ammunition), but American control of the fort would prevent British reinforcements in Augusta from reaching Ninety Six, which Greene was preparing to march against.

Lee's strategy was so dated that the British were ashamed to admit they had fallen for it. A detachment of Patriots under Maj. John Rudolph was sent to feign an attack and hasty retreat, drawing the British out of the stockaded fort in pursuit. With half the British force gone, the remainder of Lee's men easily captured the post and its precious booty. Major Rudolph chased the first group back and they were quickly surrounded and subdued. Lee was then free to march on Savannah.

Directions: From Jackson, go north on Hwy. 5 (Main Rd.), then left onto Bluff Landing Rd. (just past city limits near Matlock Church). Or take SR 32 (Silver Bluff Rd.) towards the river—it becomes a dirt road and converges with Bluff Landing Rd. Follow it several miles to the landing. As you face the boat landing, there are two paths leading into the woods on the left. Take either path (they converge) and walk a short distance (approximately one-quarter mile) until the path turns to the left, gently sloping uphill. This was the fort's river landing. As you enter the woods, notice the small orange flags, remnants of an archaeological dig that marks the outline of the house.

Ninety Six

Date: November 19-21, 1775, and May 22-June 19, 1781
Location: Near Ninety Six, Greenwood County
Commanders: Gen. Nathanael Greene; Col. John H. Cruger
   (1781)
Casualties: American—58k, 76w; British—27k, 58w (1781)

Ninety-Six. One of the guns used in the battle at the Star Fort.

Established in the 1730s as a trading post, the village of Ninety Six was given its odd name because it was supposedly 96 miles from the Cherokee town of Keowee.[1] By the time of the American Revolution, it was an important crossroads to and from Charleston and served as the seat of government in that part of the colony, with a courthouse, a jail, and a thriving community. During the Revolution, Ninety Six was the westernmost of the British outposts and the site of two battles.

The first battle took place early in the war, November 1775. Tensions between Patriots and Loyalists in the upcountry had been festering and led to civil war in the area. It would become the first Revolutionary War battle south of New England. The catalyst for the bloodshed was a supply of lead and gunpowder sent by the Patriot government in Charleston to the Cherokees, ostensibly for use in hunting. Loyalists interpreted their motives differently and seized the munitions. Local Patriot leader Maj. Andrew Williamson had already ordered the arrest of local Loyalist leader Robert Cunningham and sent him to Charleston; he now ordered his followers to recapture the ammunition. When he learned that a force of Loyalists, under the command of Cunningham's brother Patrick, was three times the size of his own force of 600 men and headed his way, Williamson had a stockade hastily constructed near the Ninety Six courthouse, where he was determined to make his stand.

And stand he did. The fighting began when two of his men were seized outside the fort during negotiations. Fighting was heavy but sporadic for three days, during which the Patriots suffered from a shortage of both water and gunpowder. Finally, when news reached Cunningham that reinforcements were on their way to the Patriots, he arranged a treaty that would let their superiors settle their differences. When Patriot colonel Richard Richardson arrived with his men, he considered the agreement nonbinding, as he had neither negotiated nor signed it. He managed to capture several Loyalist leaders and send them to Charleston under arrest. He went on to move against Patrick Cunningham's camp. Fighting was just beginning in the upcountry.

The second battle of Ninety Six took place five and one-half years later. By this time, the British had erected a fort in the shape of an eight-sided star. It had become a stronghold against which Patriot forces had been unsuccessful. The Star Fort was under the command of Col. John H. Cruger, who had about 550 men in the seemingly impregnable fortress. But American generals like Nathanael Greene and Francis Marion had been capturing British outposts one by one in recent months—some of them (like Camden) falling even when the British won the battle. In fact, several messengers had been sent to Ninety Six with orders for Cruger to abandon the post, but all the messengers had been captured by the Americans. With the Patriots on their way, Cruger fortified the post with a ravine, abatis, and small stockade to protect his water supply. General Greene arrived on May 22 and immediately lay siege to the Star Fort.

Greene tried many tactics to force a surrender. Under the advice of his engineer, Thaddeus Kosciuszko, a mine tunnel was dug, but the operation was discovered and the diggers were bayoneted by the enemy. Several zigzag lines of trenches were dug to slowly advance on the fort in a more traditional approach, but while this work was proceeding, Greene also tried a 30-foot-tall log Maham's Tower. It proved futile, as the British simply heightened the walls of the fort with sandbags. Also futile was the use of fire arrows; the British ripped the roofs off susceptible buildings as the arrows flew overhead. Greene did manage to interrupt the water supply, and when Cruger could not find water by digging a well, he sent naked Negroes out at night to fetch water from a nearby stream.

After a month-long siege, Greene became impatient, especially when he learned that Lord Rawdon was on his way with 2,000 reinforcements. Greene reluctantly approved a plan devised by his troops for a frontal assault from his closest trenches. However, the attack became suicidal to the Patriots due to the unique shape of the fort—no matter which side they approached, they would be caught in the crossfire between points of the star. The men were using long, hooked poles to tear down the sandbags, but they were no match for muskets and bayonets. Despite superior numbers, the Americans suffered heavy losses and Greene was forced to abandon the attack. Rawdon arrived two days later. He pursued Greene briefly but eventually had to head for Charleston. Cruger was to join him and burned the fort and stockades before abandoning Ninety Six. Once again, the Americans lost the battle, but the British were still in retreat.

Directions: From Ninety Six, go 2 miles south on Hwy. 248 to the park entrance on the left.

Quinby Bridge

Date: July 17, 1781
Location: Near Huger, Berkeley County
Commanders: Generals Francis Marion and Thomas Sumter,
  Col. Henry Lee; Lt. Col. John Coates
Casualties: American—30k, 30w; British—7k, 39w

By the summer of 1781, British outposts in South Carolina had been falling like dominoes for months and now they were reduced to a few posts around Charleston. Lt. Col. John Coates was the commander at Moncks Corner, 30 miles northwest of Charleston, but with Thomas Sumter breathing down his neck, he began his retreat. His first stop was Biggin Church (see index), which unfortunately was being used as a storehouse by the British. Coates torched the building at 3 a.m., to prevent the Americans from capturing the supplies, and fell back to Quinby Bridge.

By this time, Lighthorse Harry Lee and Francis Marion had joined Sumter's forces. It was Lee's cavalry that first reached the bridge and, once across, his lead brigade caused great panic among the British infantry. The Americans had been secure in the knowledge that, once across, the rear guard would remove the planks of the bridge, but in their haste the boards were loosened. As later-arriving reinforcements attempted to cross, the planks fell into the river and Lee's forces became separated. Deadly hand-to-hand fighting took place before Lee was able to ford the river and reorganize his troops.

The British then took up a position several miles downstream at Shubrick's Plantation. The men hid in and behind the house, outbuildings, and fences and waited for the Americans. Lee and Marion decided the position was too strong to engage in a frontal assault without Sumter's artillery, which had not yet arrived. Sumter overruled them, however, and the results were disastrous. After a useless carnage that lasted nearly three hours, the Patriot forces retreated to the newly repaired Quinby Bridge. Lee and Marion, disgusted at Sumter's irresponsible sacrifice of their men, withdrew their remaining troops, leaving Sumter alone to watch the British escape unmolested to Charleston. This would be Sumter's last battle.

Directions: From Moncks Corner, take Hwy. 402 south to Huger. Continue south on Hwy. 41 for 0.5 mile. Turn right onto SR 98 and go 0.5 mile to the bridge.

Eutaw Springs

Date: September 8, 1781
Location: Eutawville, Orangeburg County
Commanders: Gen. Nathanael Greene; Lt. Col. Alexander
 Stewart
Casualties: American—138k, 375w, 41c & m; British—85k,
 351w, 257m

Eutaw Springs. Grave of Major Majoribanks.

By early fall of 1781, all the British outposts in the midlands of the state had been captured by the Americans and the British army was inching back closer and closer to its home base in Charleston. Lt. Col. Alexander Stewart was now in command, having taken over for Lord Rawdon, who returned to England due to illness. The American army under Greene

101

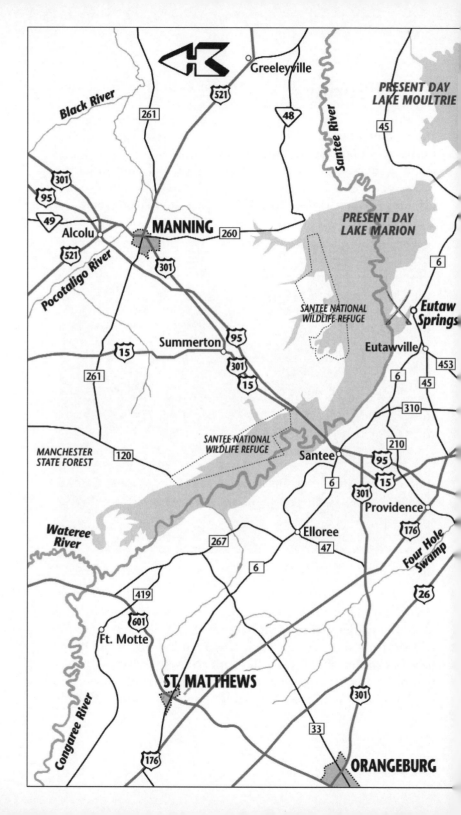

included the troops of Francis Marion, Lighthorse Harry Lee, Andrew Pickens, William Washington, and Wade Hampton.[1] This illustrious and talented group was camped across the river from the British near where the Congaree and Wateree rivers join to form the Santee River, but because of recent flooding, the Americans were forced to take a rather circuitous route to get to the other side. Meanwhile, Stewart had moved his men southeast and camped at Eutaw Springs, today under the waters of Lake Marion.

The strength of each of the armies was roughly 2,200. Severe shortages of both food and cavalry, the eyes and ears of an army, forced Stewart to send out 100 unarmed men to dig sweet potatoes. The Americans were close by and easily captured all of them. Fighting began at around 9 a.m., with the British holding the southern end of the field (to the right as you face the lake from the road, with the Patriots on the left). The soldiers on this field were the cream of the crop, and fighting was fierce and relentless as the tide of battle turned several times. Casualties began to mount up all over the field, and it would be nearly four hours before the enemy line finally began to waver. British major John Majoribanks (pronounced "Marshbanks") was in command of the only part of the British line that held while the Americans rushed forward towards their encampment. Artillery was brought up to help capture the large brick Eutaw House, where British sharpshooters were holed up.

With the taste of victory on their lips, the Patriots streamed into the British camp and came upon their supplies. As the men began to loot, eat, and drink, Majoribanks reorganized his men and launched a spectacular counterattack. Snipers in the house were able to pick off the artillerymen, and the American guns were captured. Once again, Greene had to withdraw. Casualties were heavy—almost 700 for the British, including Majoribanks, who was buried elsewhere and reinterred on the field many years later. Over 500 Americans fell, including Pickens and Washington, who were both wounded, the latter also captured. Though technically a British victory, they once again retreated towards Charleston, their ranks now decimated. One month later, Cornwallis surrendered at Yorktown.

Directions: From Eutawville, take Hwy. 6 east for 3 miles to the battlefield on the left.

Hayes Station

Date: November 19, 1781
Location: Near Joanna, Laurens County
Commanders: Col. Joseph Hayes; Capt. William Cunningham
Casualties: American—19k

Hayes Station. Foliage hides the monument commemorating the Patriots murdered here.

Cornwallis's surrender failed to bring peace to South Carolina. Particularly bitter was the Loyalist partisan leader, Capt. William ("Bloody Bill") Cunningham, who was known for his slaughter of prisoners of war. He had just perpetrated this form of murder at Cloud's Creek and was now heading for a small American post at Edgehill Plantation commanded by

Col. Joseph Hayes. Cunningham arrived at Hayes Station with a band of 300 men and warned that if any shots were fired, he would kill all 40 men inside the fortified house. In defiance, a shot was fired, killing one of Cunningham's men. "Bloody Bill" demanded a surrender, stating that if the Americans resisted, no quarter would be given. Hayes was unwilling to give up without a fight, but when the British set the house on fire with flaming arrows, he had little choice.

Hayes and another man were hanged, but the pole holding the rope broke, so Cunningham finished them off with his sword. Another Patriot who took part in the fatal whipping of Cunningham's brother met the same fate. In all, 14 men were murdered after the surrender. Pursued by angry Americans, Cunningham rode his horse to death while making his escape to Charleston. Legend has it that the animal was given a funeral with full military honors.

Directions: From Cross Hill, take Hwy. 659 (Pucketts Ferry Rd.) east. Turn right onto Hwy. 30 for 1.2 miles, left onto SR 38 (Jefferson Davis Rd.) for 1.6 miles, and right onto SR 46 for 1 mile. Go over the bridge, then left onto Williams Rd. to the end of the pavement (0.5 mile). Walk past the gate and straight up the path about 0.25 mile to the marker, which is enclosed in a small iron fence.

Fair Lawn

Date: November 27, 1781
Location: Moncks Corner, Berkeley County
Commanders: Colonels Isaac Shelby, Hezekiah Maham;
   Captain McLean
Casualties: British—150c

After the surrender at Yorktown, large numbers of Continental soldiers were dispatched to South Carolina to help send the last of the British forces back to Charleston and on to England. In addition, nearly 600 over-mountain men who had fought at Kings Mountain augmented Francis Marion's brigade, so Greene directed his amassed forces against Fair Lawn, a British post a few miles east of Moncks Corner. The plantation was originally granted to Sir Peter Colleton, eldest son of one of the original eight lords proprietors, Sir John Colleton. The estate was so large that it was a small village in of itself, with outbuildings, mills, and a landing on the Cooper River, which was protected by a redoubt. The British were using the large brick mansion house as a hospital.

The redoubt fort was guarded by 50 men under the command of a Captain McLean but was soon fortified by reinforcements who had seen the Americans on their way to Fair Lawn. When Marion arrived, he sent some of the over-mountain men under Maham and Shelby to storm the house first, expecting that McLean would leave the protection of the redoubt fort and fight in the open. Badly outnumbered, McLean refused to be lured from his stronghold and allowed about 150 British soldiers and doctors to be taken prisoner. Those who were able were marched off; those who were too ill to be moved were paroled. The Patriots also captured a good deal of supplies and arms here.

What happened next is certain—the Colleton House burned to the ground. How it happened is a mystery, with each side blaming the other. Several theories and justifications have

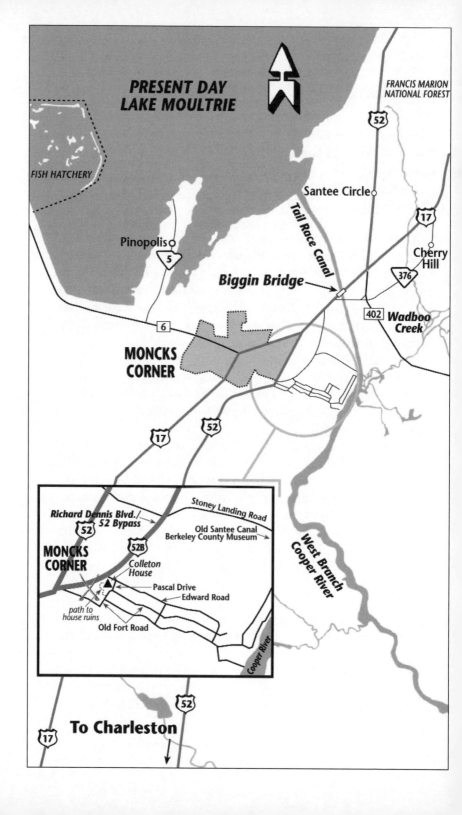

been put forth, each one as plausible as the next. The senior surgeon on duty, Dr. Dowse, testified at a court of inquiry that the house was in flames no more than 20-30 minutes after the Americans first arrived. Colonels Maham and Shelby, on the other hand, claim that they were the last men to leave and there was no sign of smoke or fire at that time. The Colleton family held the British responsible.

Directions: From Richard Dennis Blvd. (bypass for Hwy. 52, east of Moncks Corner), turn onto Edward Rd. (0.5 mile south of Stoney Landing Rd., which is the entrance to the Old Santee Canal and Berkeley County Museum), then right onto Pascal Dr. Park halfway down this street on the right and look for a path into the woods just ahead of where you've parked. This path is strewn with the brick remains of the old Colleton House. Continue along the path, which brings you back to Pascal Dr., just below Old Fort Rd.

Warning! *Copperhead snakes are the same color as old bricks and they like to hide among and under them. Disturbing their brick homes can be hazardous or deadly! (Please leave the remaining foundation of the Colleton home intact.)*

Fort Dorchester

Date: December 1, 1781
Location: Near Summerville, Dorchester County
Commanders: Gen. Nathanael Greene, Col. Wade Hampton
Casualties: British—50k & w

Fort Dorchester. The original tabby walls have survived the centuries.

Only 25 miles from Charleston, Fort Dorchester was one of the last outposts to fall before the British retreated all the way to Charleston. Built in 1757, the fort boasted eight-foot-high tabby walls[1] enclosing the brick powder magazine and was occupied early in the war by Patriots under the command of Capt. Francis Marion. The fort fell to the British after they occupied

Charleston. It served as a vital supply line, as it is located at the navigational head of the Ashley River.

In December 1781, Greene thought it was time to take the fort from the British once and for all. While marching towards an encampment at Round O, he sent 400 cavalry and infantry under Col. Wade Hampton against more than twice that number at Fort Dorchester. Loyalists in the area had warned the commander there of the Patriots' approach, but when the attack failed to materialize, 50 men who were sent out to reconnoiter ran into Hampton's cavalry. Only a few British survived the ensuing skirmish, but they managed to convince their commander that Greene's entire army was upon them. Unwilling to do battle, the British destroyed any supplies they could not carry, threw the cannon into the Ashley River, and retreated to Charleston under cover of night.

Directions: The entrance to Old Dorchester State Park is off Hwy. 642 (Dorchester Rd.), about 25 miles northwest of Charleston and 0.5 mile past Trolley Rd.

Videau's Bridge

Date: January 3, 1782
Location: Between Huger and Cainhoy, Berkeley County
Commanders: Col. Richard Richardson; Maj. John Coffin
Casualties: American—57k, 20c; British—1k, 1w

With the British holed up in Charleston and in desperate need of food for their horses, a foraging party under Maj. John Coffin was sent out by Gen. Alexander Leslie, then in command of the city. American Col. Richard Richardson was keeping close watch on the enemy's movements and immediately requested reinforcements to pursue them. Coffin and his 350 infantry and cavalry made it to Father Smith's plantation on the Cooper River just south of French Quarter Creek. Coffin sent a scouting party across Videau's Bridge while resting the remainder of his force. Meanwhile, Richardson managed to get ahead of them. Approaching the bridge from the north, his advance clashed with Coffin's scouts, who were initially repulsed. Unfortunately, many of the Patriots were raw, untrained recruits who quickly became disorganized. They were soon routed by the British, with heavy casualties. The pursuit continued for six miles, and the British were able to forage as far as Quinby Bridge before returning to Charleston.

Directions: From Huger, take Hwy. 41 south and turn right onto SR 98, crossing over Quinby Bridge. Proceed 6 miles; SR 98 crosses French Quarter Creek at Videau's Bridge.

Wambaw Bridge

Date: February 24, 1782
Location: Near McClellanville, Charleston County
Commanders: Col. Peter Horry; Col. Benjamin Thomson
Casualties: American—40k, 7c

The election of military leaders to political office was common practice in the eighteenth century, and as the 1782 session of the South Carolina General Assembly opened in Jacksonboro (Charleston was still occupied by the British), Francis Marion took his seat as senator from the parish of St. John Berkeley. He placed his brigade under the command of Col. Peter Horry who moved the men to the confluence of the Santee River and Wambaw Creek. With Marion in the legislature was Col. Hezekiah Maham, whose own brigade was camped at Mepkin Plantation on the Cooper River. When word reached the commanders that the British were taking advantage of their absence and moving out of Charleston towards the Patriot position, the Assembly finally excused them. Heretofore, it was feared that if they left, other legislators would follow them, forcing the Assembly to adjourn due to lack of a quorum.

Marion and Maham had made it as far as Mepkin Plantation when fighting broke out at the bridge over Wambaw Creek. The British were 500 strong and under the command of Col. Benjamin Thomson. Although his infantry and cavalry had doubled up on the horses in order to make the trip in one day, they were ready for battle. Horry had about the same number but was absent himself at his nearby plantation across the Santee, probably due to illness, and left Col. Adam McDonald in charge. When word of the British advance was relayed to the various regimental commanders, who were just sitting down to dinner, they were either incredulous or just slow to form their men in ranks. Those who did make it over the bridge met up with the initial brunt of the attack, and the new recruits immediately

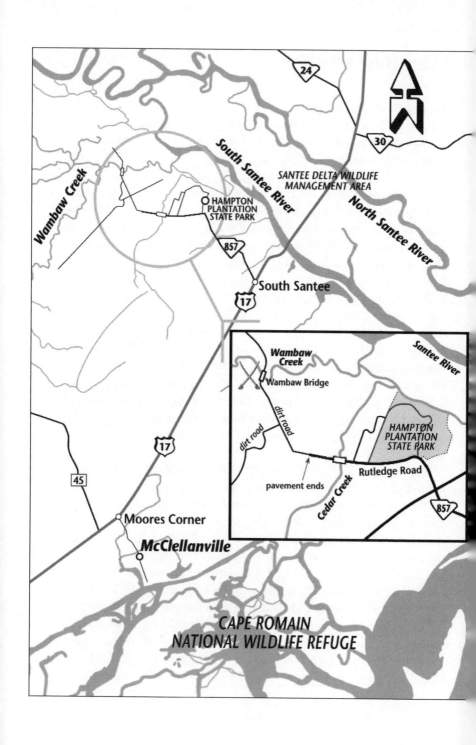

24

30

South Santee River

SANTEE DELTA WILDLIFE
MANAGEMENT AREA

North Santee River

Wambaw Creek

HAMPTON
PLANTATION
STATE PARK

857

South Santee

17

Wambaw
Creek

Santee River

Wambaw Bridge

dirt road

dirt road

HAMPTON
PLANTATION
STATE PARK

pavement ends

Cedar Creek

Rutledge Road

857

17

45

Moores Corner

McClellanville

CAPE ROMAIN
NATIONAL WILDLIFE REFUGE

broke and streamed back to the south side of Wambaw Creek. Their commander, Maj. John James, is said to have leaped a gap in the bridge that had been torn up as the Continentals rushed back over with the British on their heels. The rest of the Americans also fell back leaving 40 dead behind them.

The following day, Thomson was again able to rout the Americans, whom he found camped at Tidyman's Plantation, a few miles south of Wambaw Bridge. By now, Marion had arrived but ordered Capt. John Smith to lead the attack against the British, who were in the process of driving a herd of captured cattle to Charleston. Smith's inexperienced men were scattered by enemy fire when they broke ranks to get around a pond. Some of the fleeing men tried to escape by swimming across the Santee River but became easy targets for British sharpshooters. The British claimed they killed 20 and captured 12 as they made off with the beef.

Directions: From McClellanville, take Hwy. 17 north for approximately 7 miles. Turn left onto Rutledge Rd. at the sign to Hampton Plantation State Park (SR 857). Go 1.4 miles past the park entrance to where the pavement ends and continue on the dirt road for 1 mile to the bridge. If the gate is closed, park and walk the remaining 0.2 mile to the bridge.

Dean Swamp

Date: May 1782
Location: Near Salley, Aiken County
Commanders: Captains Michael Watson, William Butler
Casualties: American—2k, 8w

Dean Swamp. The story of this battle, also known as John Town, is inscribed on the four faces of this monument.

Here at a settlement once known as John Town, British and Loyalist prisoners were held in two bullpens. In May 1782, a band of British partisans, part of William ("Bloody Bill") Cunningham's force, set out to liberate them. Gen. Andrew Pickens assigned a contingent of militia under Captains Michael Watson and William Butler to intercept them.

Although the Patriots' approach had been detected, Watson and Butler advanced and were ambushed on the edge of Dean Swamp, with Watson being mortally wounded in the attack. Short of ammunition and outnumbered two to one, the Americans pressed forward in a final desperate charge under the leadership of Butler. This valiant decision turned the tide of battle and the British were sent fleeing to the safety of the swamp. Watson died the next day and was buried in Orangeburg.

Although Cornwallis had formally surrendered at Yorktown, Virginia on October 19, 1781, fighting in South Carolina continued until November 1782—six months after the engagement at Dean Swamp. The British did not evacuate Charleston until December 14, 1782.

Directions: From Salley, take Hwy. 394 west for 1.2 miles to where SR 52 (Voyager Rd.) converges from the right; the monument is on the right.

Francis Marion's Grave

Location: Near Pineville, Berkeley County

*The grave of Gen. Francis Marion. The sarcophagus was replaced in 1893. The
general's wife is buried beside him.*

The Swamp Fox was born in 1732 and died February 27,
1795, and is buried here at Belle Isle Plantation, home of his
brother Gabriel. There are no visible remains of the home.
Marion's own plantation, Pond Bluff, is 15 miles up the Santee
River and now under the waters of Lake Marion. Francis
Marion is buried in the raised sarcophagus, with his wife beside
him. Both graves were originally the same, but a falling tree

crushed the general's and it was replaced by the state of South Carolina in 1893. The other graves are of descendants. On the side of Marion's tomb is one of the most moving tributes to South Carolina's famous Revolutionary son:

> Sacred to the memory of General Francis Marion who depart-
> ed this life on the 27th of February, 1795 in the 63rd year of
> his age, deeply regretted by all his fellow citizens. History will
> record his worth and rising generations embalm his memory
> as one of the most distinguished Patriots and Heroes of the
> American Revolution which elevated his native country to
> honor and independence and secured to her the blessings of
> liberty and peace. This tribute of veneration and gratitude is
> erected in commemoration of the noble and disinterested
> virtues of the citizen and the gallant exploits of the soldier
> who lived without fear and died without reproach.

Directions: From St. Stephen, take Hwy. 45 west for approximately 10 miles. The entrance to the site is on the right.

Col. William Washington's grave is also in South Carolina. Although a Virginian by birth, he is buried in Charleston County. According to tradition, Colonel Washington met his future wife, Jane Elliott, when he stopped at her family's plantation home on his way to the Battle of Eutaw Springs. He had no flag for his command, so Miss Elliott made him one from a damask curtain. After their marriage, Mrs. Washington presented the banner, known as the Eutaw Flag, to the Washington Light Infantry. Colonel and Mrs. Washington are buried in the Elliott family burial ground.

Directions: From Charleston, follow Hwy. 17 south to Main Rd. (which leads to Johns Island, Kiawah Island, and Seabrook Island). Continue on Hwy. 17 for 1.7 miles to Rantowles Creek Bridge. The highway marker is on the right. Turn right onto SR 1840 (Waldon Rd.) for 0.3 mile to the end. Park where the pavement ends and walk straight ahead to the sign for the gravesite. At the sign, turn right and walk straight for about 100 feet to the small cemetery, which is surrounded by a brick fence. The Elliott plantation was nearby.

Notes

Preface

1. For an example of civil war in America, refer to the battle of Kings Mountain in upcountry South Carolina. It took place between Americans under one government. Of the nearly 3,000 men engaged, the only Brit on the field was the Loyalists' commander, Patrick Ferguson.

Fort Moultrie

1. It is for this reason that the palmetto tree is the centerpiece of South Carolina's state flag.

2. Fort Sumter was later constructed on this sandbar.

3. Legend has it that this is the origin for the aphorism, "We beat the pants off them."

Port Royal Island

1. Two signers of the Declaration of Independence were members of this battalion—Thomas Heyward, Jr., and Edward Rutledge.

Biggin Bridge

1. Many historians believe that 400 horses is an exaggeration on Tarleton's part.

Lenud's Ferry

1. See Biggin Bridge.

Buford's Bloody Battleground

1. Unbeknownst to the British, Rutledge would part company with Buford at the home of Col. Henry Rugeley, a known Tory with "a foot in both camps" who had warned his guest of the impending British arrival just in time for him to escape.

2. One of the local women who helped nurse the wounded was Elizabeth Hutchinson Jackson, mother of future president Andrew Jackson. She died later in the war from a fever contracted while nursing relatives held on prison ships in Charleston harbor and is buried on the campus of the College of Charleston.

Beckhamville

1. You will note that the date and spellings of names on the marker pictured differ from those cited in this guide. Some historical sources

give June 6 as the date, and this is supported by most research. The name spellings in this guide were likewise chosen after weighing all available evidence.

Gowen's Old Fort
1. True to his name, Bates had a reputation similar to that of William ("Bloody Bill") Cunningham.

Camden
1. He died three days later and is buried on the grounds of Bethesda Presbyterian Church on DeKalb St. (Hwy. 34) in Camden.
2. Only 700 men made it back to North Carolina.

Black Mingo Creek
1. In the future, Marion would cover planked bridges with blankets before crossing.

Kings Mountain
1. Named for the King family that lived at the foot of the mountain, not the royal forces assembled there.
2. Patrick Ferguson had been promoted from major to colonel just before the battle of Kings Mountain, but he had not yet gotten word of it. Therefore, he considered himself a major and was addressed as such. His marker gives him the rank he had attained at the time of his death. Almost all literature on this battle still refers to him as a major.
3. Ironically, the outcome of the battle might have been dramatically different if Ferguson's breech-loading rifle had been used. Although it had proven successful at Brandywine, military officials had the guns placed in storage rather than being issued to British troops.
4. These prisoners were marched north, where some were tried, 30 sentenced to death, and nine hanged.

Fishdam Ford
1. Wemyss's reputation for brutality to prisoners and civilians was second only to Tarleton's. He burned the Indiantown Presbyterian Church because he felt that, as a non-Episcopalian church, it must have been "a sedition shop."

Blackstock's Ford
1. Mary Dillard, who lived on a nearby farm and had seen Tarleton split his forces, rode off to alert Sumter.

Long Cane

1. A Major Lindsay received saber wounds to his head and arms and had one of his hands cut off as he lay wounded on the battlefield.

Cowpens

1. A first cousin to Daniel Boone and veteran of the French and Indian War, Morgan had demonstrated his military skill at Boston and Saratoga and had endured the winter with George Washington at Valley Forge.

Mount Hope Swamp

1. This took place where Hwy. 377 crosses the river, several miles south of Kingstree. There is a highway marker at the 377/521 fork.

Fort Watson

1. The mound is now on the shores of Lake Marion.

Fort Motte

1. Tradition has it that Mrs. Motte was living at her brother's home, the Miles Brewton House, when Cornwallis took it over for his headquarters and that she hid her three daughters in the attic to protect them from the advances of the British soldiers.

Ninety Six

1. Historians now dispute this, as it is actually 78 miles from Keowee. See *96 Decoded,* by David P. George, for another theory.

Eutaw Springs

1. Wade Hampton, whose brother was Capt. Edward Hampton, was the grandfather of the War for Southern Independence general, Wade Hampton.

Fort Dorchester

1. Tabby was a common 18th-century lowcountry building material made from oyster shells, lime, and sand mixed with salt water.

For Further Reading

South Carolina Department of Archives and History:

Lipscomb, Terry. *Battles, Skirmishes, and Actions of the American Revolution in South Carolina*. 1991.

———. *South Carolina Revolutionary War Battles*. Vol. 1, *The Carolina Lowcountry, April 1775-June 1776 and the Battle of Fort Moultrie*. 1994.

South Carolina Highway Historical Marker Guide. 1992.

General Histories:

Chidsey, Donald. *The War in the South: The Carolinas and Georgia in the American Revolution, An Informal History*. New York: Crown, 1969.

Hilborn, Nat and Sam. *Battleground of Freedom: South Carolina in the Revolution*. Columbia, S.C.: Sandlapper, 1970.

Lumpkin, Henry. *From Savannah to Yorktown: The American Revolution in the South*. Columbia, S.C.: University of South Carolina Press, 1981.

McCrady, Edward. *The History of South Carolina in the Revolution: 1775-1783*. 2 vols. New York: Russell & Russell, 1901-2.

Morrill, Dan L. *Southern Campaigns of the American Revolution*. Baltimore: The Nautical and Aviation Publishing Company of America, 1993.

Ramsay, David. *History of the Revolution in South Carolina*. 2 vols. Trenton: 1785.

Ripley, Warren. *Battleground: South Carolina in the Revolution*. Charleston: Post and Courier, 1983.

Symonds, Craig. *A Battlefield Atlas of the American Revolution*. Annapolis: The Nautical and Aviation Publishing Company of America, 1986.

Weigley, Russell F. *The Partisan War: The South Carolina Campaign of 1780-1782*. Columbia, S.C.: University of South Carolina Press, 1970.

Many counties publish their own local histories. These valuable resources can often be obtained through county historical societies. The South Carolina Department of Archives and History publishes the annual *Directory of South Carolina Historical Organizations*, which lists current contacts in each county.

Index